Rescue Plan
for
Planet Earth

Democratic World Government
through a
Global Referendum

The world faces a true planetary emergency. Former U.S. vice-president Al Gore (and now Nobel Laureate) in testimony to committees of the House of Representatives and Senate, March 21, 2007

The concept of world government should be looked at in a new millennium as part of a grown-up and sensible discussion. Press release on Harold S. Bidmead's books, *Parliament of Man* (1992) and *Tilting at Windbags: The Autobiography of a World Federalist* (2005)

The earth is not dying, it is being killed. And the people who are killing it have names and addresses. Utah Phillips, singer, storyteller, archivist, historian, activist, philosopher, radio show host

If leaders won't lead, let the people lead, and the leaders will surely follow. Benjamin B. Ferencz, *New Legal Foundations for Global Survival*, 1994

All truth passes through three states: First, it is ridiculed. Second, it is violently opposed. And third, it is accepted as self-evident. Andrew Schopenhauer, German philosopher (1788 - 1860)

There is nothing easier than lopping off heads and nothing harder than developing ideas. Fyodor Dostoevsky

Rescue Plan
for
Planet Earth

Democratic World Government
through a
Global Referendum

Jim Stark

The Key Publishing House Inc.

First Edition 2008
The Key Publishing House Inc.
Toronto, Canada
Website: www.thekeypublish.com
E-mail: info@thekeypublish.com

ISBN 978-0-9782526-5-6 paperback

Cover design Olga Lagounova
The cover design was inspired by a view of the Earth as seen by the Apollo 17 crew traveling toward the moon. Photograph source: NASA

Published in association with Stalets Literary Agency, Nashville, TN.

Library and Archives Canada Cataloguing in Publication
Stark, Jim,
Rescue plan for planet Earth : democratic world government through a global referendum / Jim Stark.
Originally published under title: Democratic world government through a global referendum.
Includes bibliographical references and index.
ISBN 978-0-9782526-5-6
JZ1308.S73 2008   321'.04   C2007-907250-X

Printed and bound by MCRL in China. This book is printed on paper suitable for recycling and made from fully sustained forest sources.

The Key Publishing promotes mutual understanding, respect and peaceful coexistence among the people of the world. We represent unique and unconventional voices whose objective is to bring peace, harmony, and happiness to our human society.

The Key Publishing House Inc.

ADVANCE PRAISE FOR
THE CONCEPT AND THE AUTHOR

Jim, I've always admired your total commitment and your passion. We need millions more like you. *David Suzuki, David Suzuki Foundation, Canada*

It's about time someone did this. All great visionary ideas seem mad or utopian—until they become reality. A global referendum on whether we, the people of the world, wish to democratically govern ourselves is about as sane a political idea as I can imagine. *Syd Baumel, Winnipeg, Manitoba, National Council member, World Federalists Movement—Canada*
Brilliant idea, Jim. *Robert Bernstein, Canadian physician*

Love the idea. Keep up the wonderful work. *Brian Coughlan, a "world citizen" from Sweden*

Thank you for … your idea for a global referendum. Mr. Annan has asked me to convey his admiration for your enthusiasm and energy, and sends you his best wishes for the success of your endeavour. *Ruth McCoy, on behalf of Kofi Annan, former Secretary-General of the United Nations*

Today we live in a globalised but anarchic world of sovereign nation states, in which the lack of effective global governance ensures the dominance of military and economic might over justice and law. The proposal for a global referendum on democratic world government offers a desperately-needed opportunity to save ourselves from the inevitable and ultimately terminal conflicts of a world system based on competition rather than cooperation, an escape from the looming disasters of climate change, resource depletion, overpopulation, injustice, poverty and runaway military expenditures. *Hugh Steadman, President, Sapiens*

Jim Stark's wonderful idea deserves our full support. *Raj Shekhar Chandola, Head of the World Unity and Peace Education Department at City Montessori School in Lucknow, India*

DEDICATIONS

To Edie Nims (née Ivory),
without whose faith and able hand there might be no
online global referendum for a democratic world government.

* * *

To the people of the world,
in the hope that we will succeed where nations have failed
so that this generation's legacy to its children may be
a world without war,
a just and sustainable global village.

ACKNOWLEDGEMENTS

My deepest appreciation to my dear, patient and funny wife, Earleen Devine, without whose enduring love and support I would resemble toast. Thanks also to my terrific parents-in-law, Daisy and (the late) Earl Devine, for their years of support, and to my stepson Martin Gregory for his advice. I am indebted to David Wright, who did the legal research needed for Chapter 10 and wrote Chapter 14. My thanks to the founder and president of Sapiens in New Zealand, Hugh Steadman, who did an analysis of the book that led me to rethink key issues. My thanks to all those who read early drafts of the manuscript and advised me, including Deryl Thompson, Maureen Green and Larry Kazdan, and especially my literary agent and friend, Ted Stalets. I am very grateful to Dr. Huda Henry-Riyad, CEO of The Key Publishing House Inc. Her mission statement (near the bottom of page iv) is truly to be admired, and it is what brought me to submit my book to The Key. And finally, my appreciation to all those who voted in the fledgling global referendum … and if you are not included in that number yet, you could always vote now, or soon, at www.voteworldgovernment.org.

THE ORGANIZATION BEHIND THE BOOK

"**Vote World Government**" is a non-profit organization registered in July, 2004, in Québec, Canada as "VWG.org." Our Internet site is www.voteworldgovernment.org. You can get in touch with us by clicking on the "Contact Us" link or by writing us at: **Vote World Government, P.O. Box 1102, Shawville, Québec, Canada J0X 2Y0**. Vote World Government is not affiliated with any political party, religion or ideology.

BOXED QUOTATIONS

Throughout the book, there are quotations in boxes. I wanted to let you know that many important and wise people have said things that support the ideas presented here.

Table of Contents

ABOUT FOOTNOTES

Some people just don't like footnotes, but many readers appreciate them. If you are in the first group, please forgive me and move on. You don't have to read them, after all.

Introduction

A book covering all aspects of Earth's very serious crisis plus the obvious political fix, a democratic world government, would be the size of a big-city telephone directory. Many books have already been written about the need to globalize democracy and about the structure and function of a theoretical global government and world parliament. The problem is that no one has yet devised a credible strategy that can get us from the current anarchy among nations to the democratically governed world that we so desperately need. I have come to the conclusion that a global referendum is a realistic strategy that can get the job done ... *if* the human race has the good sense to do it and to vote "yes," that is.

After WWI, we created the League of Nations ... and we got it wrong. After WWII, we created the United Nations ... and we got it wrong *again*! During and after the Cold War, some voices were raised for "UN reform," but nothing substantial is happening, or is likely to happen. With more than 80 countries actively involved in the so-called war on terror, WWIII may not be too far into the future. Some day soon, we simply have to get things done right and create the democratic institution through which we can make and enforce world law and govern ourselves globally, just as we now do within our democratic nations, provinces and municipalities.

While this book anticipates and encourages the involvement of national governments in the process and recognizes the undoubted desirability of such involvements at the earliest possible moment, I must stress that it is essential for *the people* to effectively call the shots at each step along the way. The nations and bureaucrats had their chances, and they failed, utterly. It is now the turn and the responsibility of the people of the world to see if we can get it done right, and thus save our wonderful planet, and ourselves, from extinction.

The initiative proposed is based first on the ability of individual human beings to create an irresistible tsunami of "people-power." But it is also an attempt to build on the lessons learned from the so-called Ottawa Process, whereby national governments worked with civil society (a collective term meaning, in this case, more than 1,000 non-governmental organizations, or NGOs) to address a problem of common concern, and succeeded in putting in place, in record time, a treaty banning landmines which is now adhered to by most nations.

There appears to be a consensus among both the nations and the people of Earth (and some corporate leaders) that there now exist *very* dangerous problems requiring *urgent* global action in the areas of security and the environment. What we lack is a consensus on the solutions to these problems, and that consensus has to be found before we destroy ourselves.

The band-aid solutions applied by individual nations or groups of aligned nations are not working, nor should they be expected to work. The root problems are what must be addressed, and many of these can *only* be solved on a worldwide basis. We have to stop squandering limited resources on failed solutions, and work instead to develop an effective institution that can deliver comprehensive programs that can be applied globally. Only then will humanity succeed in solving the many problems we have created, problems that now threaten to annihilate us.

Given the current anarchy among the nations, the tool we need to address worldwide problems is a democratically elected world parliament. The global referendum initiative, launched by an NGO called Vote World Government, is the right and necessary first step along the road to that goal. A world parliament is an idea whose time has finally come. We think humanity can make it a reality in time to save ourselves. The environmental, peace, human rights and social justice movements, if they were united in a common cause against self-destruction, do have the power to mobilize the world's peoples and stir their governments into acting.

This is an invitation to individuals to make things happen in a new way that hadn't been thought of before. It is also an invitation to all elements in civil society to come together, as a new part of their ongoing efforts in their particular spheres, to mobilize their members and supporters to actively participate in this initiative. Together, we can establish a world parliament where all our concerns will be heard, a world government that will have the legitimacy, the resources and the vision to develop global solutions, and the power to carry them out.

Preface

On January 17, 2007, Dr. Stephen Hawking, the celebrated British cosmologist who has suffered from Lou Gehrig's disease (or ALS, amyotrophic lateral sclerosis) for 40 years, participated in a news conference organized by the Bulletin of the Atomic Scientists, a Chicago-based watchdog group of world class scientists who think that along with the job of inventing dangerous technologies goes a responsibility to warn humanity if these technologies pose a danger to our species' existence. Hawking communicates by twitching the one muscle he has control of—his cheek—to select words on his computer, which are then verbalized by a voice synthesizer. Using this means, he "said" the following at the news conference:

"As scientists, we understand the dangers of nuclear weapons and their devastating effects, and we are learning how human activities and technologies are affecting climate systems in ways that may forever change life on Earth. As citizens of the world, we have a duty to alert the public to the unnecessary risks that we live with every day, and to the perils we foresee if governments and societies do not take action now to render nuclear weapons obsolete and to prevent further climate change."

The question becomes: what "action" should we take to get such a difficult job done ... permanently? This book is meant to provide you with a worthy answer to that critical question.

Chapter 1

The situation

> **All truth passes through three states: First, it is ridiculed. Second, it is violently opposed. And third, it is accepted as self-evident.** Andrew Schopenhauer, German philosopher (1788 - 1860)

The human race is the most intelligent species on planet Earth, and yet here we are, sleepwalking towards omnicide. How can that be? And what can we do about it at this late date?

"Omnicide" is a fairly new word that is not in most dictionaries yet, but if you Google it, you will find 44,000+ references. It means the killing of everything, the extinction of our species—humanity, or *Homo sapiens*—and the extermination of all or most other life forms; basically the assassination of Earth.[1] Omnicide would be the ultimate crime against humanity, against life, and against whatever deity or deities may exist. If you are not aware of this clear and present danger, then you are probably not paying enough attention to the news, and by default, you may, inadvertently, have become part of the problem, one of the "bad guys," even if you are a fine person in every other respect. This lemming-march threatens to be the very last act in human history, and if you are not even aware of it, then you simply have not yet connected the dots, and as a result, you may be out of touch with reality to such an extent that your personal "disconnect" may even qualify as a mental disorder, like the affliction that befuddled Emperor Nero, who allegedly "fiddled while Rome burned."[2]

> **It's okay to be passionate about the survival of planet Earth.** Dr. Helen Caldicott, Australian physician and peace activist, at an Operation Dismantle conference in 1984

I have heard it said that "the harsher the truth, the better the friend that tells you about it." Those who don't subscribe to this maxim may find me

---

[1] See http://en.wikipedia.org/wiki/Human_extinction for more on this unhappy topic.

[2] I know this tale is historically doubtful, if only because the fiddle or violin was not invented in or before Nero's time. However, because this tale is well known, it serves charmingly to make a most un-charming point.

unduly harsh, and that is most unfortunate. I *do* subscribe to that maxim, and all I am trying to do here is hammer home the literally suicidal situation that we have gotten ourselves into as a species, and be as good a friend as I know how to be to you and to all of my fellow human beings.

> **It would indeed be the ultimate tragedy if the history of the human race proved to be nothing more noble than the story of an ape playing with a box of matches on a petrol dump.** David Ormsby-Gore, 5th Baron Harlech, Minister of State, Great Britain, in the *Christian Science Monitor*, 1960

Regarding omnicide, most people are in denial about it, so I really must be blunt, as Einstein was just after WWII, when he opined: "The unleashed power of the atom has changed everything save our modes of thinking, and we thus drift toward unparalleled catastrophe." He used the word "drift," as one might drift down a river, without any thought to one's destination and without any apparent sense of having control over one's destiny. That bleak assessment of our situation is 60 years old, and we still haven't even banned nuclear weapons, let alone war. We inhabit a planet in deep environmental trouble, *and we are the trouble*, so let's take a close-up look at the "disconnect" I mentioned above, and at our real-world situation.

> **Mankind must put an end to war or war will put an end to mankind.** U.S. President John F. Kennedy, speech to the UN, September 25, 1961

An AP Poll (March 31, 2005) reported that most Americans think that their government should cut its nuclear arsenal by about half. However, the poll also revealed that average Americans think (or "guesstimate") that the USA currently has 200 nuclear weapons in its arsenal. The U.S. stockpile is between 6,000 and 10,000 nuclear weapons.[3] *That* is what I meant by "out of touch with reality," and one of the agenda items I am attempting to shove onto centre stage is the fact that there are still more than enough nuclear weapons in the world to kill us all many times over. That is called "overkill," by the way, and I remember Dr. Helen Caldicott,[4] 20+ years ago,

---

[3] Robert S. Norris and Hans M. Kristensen. "U.S. nuclear forces, 2006," *Bulletin of the Atomic Scientists* (January/February 2005): 68-71. It is hard to be exact on this number, since the USA does not like to say exactly what it has (nor do other nations). The *world* stockpile at the time of writing (2007) is *about* 27,000.

[4] Australian physician and the star of the 1980s anti-nuclear-weapons film *If You Love This Planet*, which was labelled as "propaganda" by then-U.S. president Ronald Reagan. (The movie subsequently won an Academy Award.)

emphasizing that "overkill is not a medical term—it is a political term, and an insane one." In the real world, she noted, we can die only once, not many times over.

More and more nations (and non-state players, such as terrorist groups) are trying to acquire these "overkill" nuclear weapons in a world that is already wired to self-destruct. Also, parties who can't afford to buy such things on the black market and can't make them are looking to acquire what is sometimes referred to as "the poor man's nuke," biological or chemical weapons. These are also "weapons of mass destruction," or WMD—not as flashy as a nuclear explosion, but just as lethal. All of this is … well, in a word, "alarming." And yet most people simply are not "alarmed."

One is born into a herd of buffaloes and must be glad if one is not trampled underfoot before one's time. Albert Einstein, *Einstein, a portrait*, Thomas F. Burke (editor), p. 100 (Einstein is pointing out the danger inherent in the irrational or instinctive side of human nature.)

For decades, anti-nuclear activists and the scientists who tried to warn us about climate change have been labelled "alarmists," like that famous scaredy-cat Chicken Little,[5] who ran around screaming "The sky is falling, the sky is falling." Some well-known (and otherwise intelligent) people have gone to extremes to show how anti-war or climate change activists were a few kernels short of a cob. Yet the sad tactics of twisting the truth and just plain making things up (aka "lying") are often the hallmark of those who seek to justify the nuclear weapons aresenals, or to discredit public concern about climate change. Reverend Jerry Falwell said that global warming was "phoney baloney" in a 2007 televised sermon, adding that the debate was "alarmist," "hysterical" and "a tool of Satan" … and that global warming theory was "the greatest deception in the history of science." I remember U.S. Lieutenant-General Daniel O. Graham (back in the 1970s, he headed the American Defense Intelligence Agency) telling reporters that "If a one-megaton [nuclear] weapon would explode over this building ... and you had the good sense to start walking and got behind a lilac bush, that weapon would not hurt you."[6] In 2002, before he became the prime minister of

---

[5] Fable of unknown origin, popularized by Walt Disney in a short film in 1943. The fable is known as *Chicken Little* or *The Sky is Falling*. The character is now used to indicate an hysterical or mistaken belief that disaster is imminent.

[6] In the 1980's, I published Graham's infamous quote in *The Dismantler*, along with the following list of the effects of a one-megaton bomb. "The temperature in the middle of the blast would be in the millions of degrees. The pressure would be ten million times normal. Everything in a radius of 1 to 1.5 miles would be vaporized or otherwise demolished. Winds would move out from the blast at about 500 miles per hour. Up to 1.5 miles from the centre,

Canada, Stephen Harper said that global warming was "a money-sucking socialist scheme."[7] So, let's deal with this question of "alarmism" head on.

> **In an all-out nuclear war, more destructive power than in all of World War II would be unleashed every second during the long afternoon it would take for all the missiles and bombs to fall. A World War II every second--more people killed in the first few hours than all the wars of history put together. The survivors, if any, would live in despair amid the poisoned ruins of a civilization that had committed suicide.** Jimmy Carter, "Farewell Address to the American People," January 14, 1981

> **Everybody's going to make it** (survive a nuclear WWIII) **if there are enough shovels to go around. Dig a hole, cover it with a couple of doors and then throw three feet of dirt on top. It's the dirt that does it.** T.K. Jones, Deputy Under Secretary of Defense for Strategic and Theater Nuclear Forces, *LA Times*, January 16, 1982

> **I decline to accept the end of man.** William Faulkner, speech upon receiving the Nobel Prize, December 10, 1950

Either there is cause for alarm, or there is not, and if not, then I will have to admit that I wasted a lot of my life designing a grand solution for a problem that doesn't even exist. However, I remember that during the Cold War, we[8] tried to nail down what we'd called the "GOF," or "global overkill factor." The lowest estimate that we found (uttered by U.S. Congressman Leon Panetta) was ten. This was in the 1980s. There are fewer nukes today, but their destructive capacity has not changed significantly, so it would not be "alarmist" to go with that estimate today, and say that there are, in the early 21st century, enough nuclear weapons to assassinate humanity 10 times over. (Bear in mind that it doesn't matter greatly what the GOF is, because

---

98% of the people would be killed outright. Up to 3 miles out, 50% would be killed and 40% would be injured. At 5 to 10 miles out, 10% would be killed outright and there would still be serious injuries. Within a 5-mile radius, thermal radiation would ignite anything flammable and cook any exposed skin. There would be third degree burns 8 miles out. People who looked at the fireball of a one-megaton bomb from 10 miles away would be instantly blinded. And this is not even to mention the effects of nuclear radiation and fallout."

[7] Canadian Press, January 30, 2007. As prime minister, Conservative Stephen Harper sort-of saw the light and tried to turn a little "green," with mixed results.

[8] I headed Operation Dismantle, a Canadian nuclear disarmament organization, at the time.

after we murder ourselves once, additional detonations will do nothing but "make the rubble bounce," as Churchill said.)

Even without referring to our incredible weapons of war, the use of which can destroy the planet Earth,[9] a 2006 UN report, involving 1,360 scientists from 95 countries, states that two thirds of the resources of the planet have "already been consumed," and food, clean water and non-renewable energy supplies are vanishing at an "alarming" rate.[10] It also says that one quarter of all mammalian species may soon become extinct (plus similar percentages of birds and amphibians). By way of explanation, Jay Keller (of Population Connection) said that planet Earth "cannot sustain the six billion human beings who exist now, let alone the 7, 8, or 9 billion that we are headed towards." And Robert Watson, former Chief Scientist at the World Bank, added: "We are undermining the resources we are critically dependent on," which in my view is just another way of saying that we are "committing omnicide."

> **If the last IPCC** [the UN's Nobel Prize winning Intergovernmental Panel on Climate Change] **report was a wake up call, this one is a screaming siren.... The bad news is that the more we know, the more precarious the future looks. There's a clear message to governments here, and the window for action is narrowing fast.** Stephanie Tunmore, Greenpeace, Feb. 2007, www.blogsw.solidwastemag.com

In its "Living Planet Report" of October, 2006, the World Wildlife Fund asserts that the world's natural ecosystems are being degraded at such a rate that by 2050 we'll need *two* Earths to meet human needs, and says that "the natural health of planet Earth has declined by 30% just since 1970."[11] WWF calls this a "dangerous trend," since essential resources will be increasingly fought over by desperate nations, and hoarded by the more fortunate. In his response to the report, Princeton atmospheric scientist Michael Oppenheimer said that "civilization just won't be able to cope ... even within this century." He went on to say that we're using *five times* too much fossil fuel, and the excess has thrown the Earth dangerously out of balance through global warming, and "we have to cut greenhouse gases by

---

[9] Would it still be called "war" if we destroyed the whole planet? Doesn't a war have to come to an end, with some people on all sides surviving?

[10] The report was done by the United Nations Environment Program (et al). It is entitled *The Millennium Ecosystem Assessment*. It concludes that many of the planet's essential (to our survival) systems are endangered, mostly due to human activity. And it warns that, if left unchecked, the consequences could be "dire" (a polite way of saying we're killing ourselves, and everything else).

[11] All quotes in this paragraph are from a report on ABC News, October 24, 2006.

80%, *starting now*, to bring the Earth's system back into balance." However, human production of these greenhouse gases is going *up*, not down. "The consequences [of all this] are both predictable and dire," said James Leape, director general of WWF in the USA, meaning we can't claim we didn't know when our grandchildren ask us why we have destroyed *their* planet beyond any hope of reclamation.

> **We do not inherit the Earth from our Ancestors, we borrow it from our Children.** Ancient American Aboriginal proverb[12]

On October 30, 2006, Peter Mansbridge, the distinguished anchor of CBC TV's flagship newscast (*The National*), opened with a story under the onscreen title, "Doomsday Report." "If there's a global warming alarm out there," he began excitedly, "it is ringing tonight." He went on to describe the "sweeping" British study that put the *economic* impact of climate change on par with the Second World War or the Great Depression. "That's pretty alarming," he said. (And there's that "A"-word again ... "alarm" ... twice.)

> **Alarm bells are ringing. The world must wake up to the threat posed by climate change.** Catherine Pearce, Friends of the Earth, Feb. 2, 2007

Sir Nicholas Stern,[13] described as "one of the world's most credentialed economists," is then shown onscreen saying: "When people don't pay for the consequences of their actions, we have market failure. This is the greatest market failure the world has seen." He went on to say that if we deal with it now, it would cost perhaps 1% of the global economy. And if we procrastinate, it will cost up to 20%—a staggering seven *trillion* dollars. And that is not to mention the human suffering if "100 million people [are] forced from their homes by rising sea levels," or if we have some "tens of millions of climate refugees." And what is the response of governments and industries and all of us individuals? As mentioned above, the production of greenhouse gases is increasing, not decreasing.

---

[12] The full quote is this (choices of lower- or upper-case letters are not mine): "Treat the earth well: it was not given to you by your parents, it was loaned to you by your children. We do not inherit the Earth from our Ancestors, we borrow it from our Children." It is variously attributed as above, or to: 1) Haida proverb; 2) Ancient Indian proverb; 3) Native American proverb.

[13] Sir Nicholas Stern was then Head of the Government Economics Service and Adviser to the British Government on the economics of climate change.

> **The question is not whether climate change is happening or not, but whether, in the face of this emergency, we ourselves can change fast enough.** UN Secretary-General Kofi Annan, Nairobi, Kenya, 2006

Previous generations sought to conquer or "tame" nature in the pursuit of wealth and a better life. As a result of their success, we are now faced with an invoice for vast sums to restore nature to its previous position as an abundant "sustainer" of all life. These expenses represent the hidden cost involved in unsustainable production practices that temporarily benefited a few at the enormous expense of the many.

> **A few diehard sceptics continue to deny global warming is taking place and try to sow doubt. They should be seen for what they are: out of step, out of arguments and out of time. The scientific consensus is becoming not only more complete, but also more alarming. Many scientists long known for their caution are now saying that global warming trends are perilously close to a point of no return.** Kofi Annan, November 15, 2006

In a speech to the Canadian Nuclear Association on the Kyoto accord, Dr. James Lovelock (who is "pro nuclear power," and "no tree-hugger," by his own description) said that we "have little time left to act" on global warming[14] (*Globe and Mail*, March, 2005). He explained further: "Those who construct [computer] models of such changes ... predict that somewhere between 400 and 600 parts per million of carbon dioxide, Earth passes a threshold beyond which global warming becomes irreversible [meaning the Earth may be so different as to be inhospitable to human life]. We are now at 380 parts per million, and we could reach 400 ppm within seven years." This is one more nice, polite way of saying that we humans are committing omnicide, yet some people doggedly continue to deny the science of climate change, either because their industry would be more profitable if global warming could be dismissed as a scientific hoax, or because a malevolent or ignorant authority figure said to do so (most people simply do not have the specialized knowledge needed to assess for themselves the accuracy or value of scientific findings).

The oceans that cover about 70 percent of the Earth's surface are not doing well either. A report[15] in the prestigious journal *Science* (November 2,

---

[14] Now, most scientists prefer or insist upon the term "climate change."
[15] This research was led by Dr. Boris Worm, Dalhousie University, Nova Scotia, Canada.

2006) says that if present trends continue, all the oceans will be *essentially emptied of seafood by 2048.* Thirty percent of all fish stocks are already "in collapse" (depleted by 90% or so) because of overfishing, and remaining stocks are certain to follow unless something dramatic is done, soon. The entire oceanic ecosystem is in crisis, and on the high seas there is essentially no effective governance.[16] It seems there is no part of this planet that we humans cannot get to, and ruin ... or at least harm severely.

On January 17, 2007, the Bulletin of the Atomic Scientists[17] announced that the hands of its world famous "doomsday clock" would be pushed forward by two minutes, to the position of five minutes to midnight, meaning that at this time, the human race is in great danger of causing its own extinction—in *significantly greater danger than before.* And for the first time, they cited not only the nuclear danger (the "second nuclear age" is what they called it, as rogue states and non-state players—like al-Qaeda—seek to build, buy or steal nukes), but also the fact that we are risking omnicide through climate change. The Bulletin spokesperson did not use the word "omnicide," but he could have, and maybe should have. Language should be as precise as possible, especially for scientists, and "omnicide" is the only word that captures the scope and essence of the horrific crime[18] that we are now committing. (See Preface for more on this press conference.)

> **If we don't end war, war will end us.** H.G. Wells, English writer, *Things to Come*, 1936

I find it *embarrassing* to be a human being. Yes, I know that most of the people that we know *personally* are nice people, or at least okay, but as a group, humans are wrecking everything, soiling the nest, and not just for ourselves, but potentially for all life forms. If that isn't the absolute most embarrassing reputation to be stuck with, I don't know what is. It is far worse than any garden-variety criminal, like a car thief or a mugger. We belong to a family, and if planet Earth is regarded as the patient, then our

---

[16] There is the *Law of the Sea Treaty* and a few other international efforts, but these have not done much, or enough, to prevent or even slow the ecological disaster that is described by Dr. Worm et al.

[17] Founded back in 1945 as a newsletter for nuclear physicists concerned by the possibility of nuclear war, it is now an "organization" focused more generally on manmade threats to the survival of human civilization.

[18] Reporting from the Valencia, Spain meeting of the IPCC (November 16, 2007), BBC's environmental correspondent David Shukman said the "shocking" scientific findings had become "suddenly alarming," and that: "People here say it's screamingly obvious that action needs to be taken, some officials saying it would be *even criminally irresponsible* not to [take action]." (Emphasis added.)

family must be seen as a disease ... a global pandemic. Look anywhere, and there we are, doing harm.

On March 21, 2007, former American vice-president Al Gore[19] testified to committees of the U.S. House of Representatives and Senate. "Nature is on the run," he said. "Future generations will suffer ... and they will ask, 'What in God's name were they doing? Didn't they see the evidence? Didn't they hear the warnings?'" Yet even with his enormous TV presence and the credibility of his having won an Academy Award for the film on climate change that he starred in (*An Inconvenient Truth*) plus having been nominated for the 2007 Nobel Peace Prize (which he later won, with the IPCC), he still felt the need to half-apologize for his dire warning. "The world faces a true planetary emergency," he said, but with his next breath he added: "I know that sounds shrill, and I know it's a challenge to the moral imagination to see and feel and understand that the entire relationship between humanity and the planet has been altered."

Shrill? I think not. We *do* face a planetary emergency, just like he said.[20]

It will certainly not be easy to awaken in people a new sense of responsibility for the world, an ability to conduct themselves as if they were to live on this earth forever, and ... be held answerable for its condition one day. Vaclav Havel, writer, 1st president of Czech Republic, from "The World in our Hands," *Sunrise* magazine, October/November 1995

Stephen Hawking, the celebrated British cosmologist, is far too well known as a towering genius to be called "shrill," yet he thinks the chances that we will in fact destroy ourselves and the planet are so terrifyingly high that ... well, in his own words:

> It is important for the human race to spread out into space for the survival of the species. Life on Earth is at the ever-increasing risk of being wiped out by a disaster such as sudden global warming, nuclear war, a genetically engineered virus or other dangers we have not yet thought of. [www.openthefuture.com, June 19, 2006, Jamais Cascio's blog, "Stephen Hawking, Global Warming, and Moving Out"]

---

[19] Author of the 2007 book, *The Assault on Reason*, about George Bush's absurd approach to climate change ... and about the demise of public discourse and the "meritocracy of ideas" ... and about democracy.

[20] On April 28, 2007, Al Gore called the Canadian government's climate change policy a "complete and total fraud, designed to mislead the Canadian people." That, too, *sounds* shrill, but is it accurate? If so, then it's not really shrill, is it?

Sir Richard Branson, billionaire and founder of Virgin Airlines, says we face "an emergency far greater than WWI *and* WWII." (*Out of Gas: We Were Warned*, CNN, June 2, 2007) He also states flatly that "the world is hurtling out of control," and that "we lack the political leadership to stop it from hurtling out of control." But Branson is investing many millions of dollars in potential solutions, like cellulose ethanol fuel for cars, so surely we can't dismiss him as a disingenuous alarmist or stick him with the character flaw of being "shrill."

Steve Connor, the science editor of the *Independent* (UK), wrote a lead article (June 19, 2007) under the headline: "The Earth today stands in imminent peril." He was responding to a 29-page paper called "Climate change and trace gases," by Dr. James Hansen et al, published by the *Philosophical Transactions of the Royal Society*.[21] Hansen wrote: "We have about ten years to put into effect the draconian measures needed to curb CO_2 emissions quickly enough to avert a dangerous rise in global temperature." As for evidence to suggest that we are aware of the gravity of our situation and doing what is required of us to avert disaster, *there is none*. Connor sums up our dilemma and deals with the (anticipated) accusation that he is being "shrill" as follows:

> … nothing short of a planetary rescue will save it [the world] from the environmental cataclysm of dangerous climate change. Those are not the words of eco-warriors, but the considered opinion of a group of eminent scientists writing in a peer-reviewed scientific journal…. [These scientists say that] *civilisation itself is threatened by global warming.* (Emphasis added.)

These scientists say that: "If we have not already passed the dangerous level, the energy infrastructure now in place ensures that we will pass it within several decades…. We conclude that a feasible strategy for planetary rescue almost surely requires a means of extracting [greenhouse gases] from the air." (I would add that a feasible strategy for planetary rescue also needs a political dimension, and as you may already realize, that is exactly where democratic world government comes in.)

These scientists go even further, and say that: "Humanity cannot afford to burn the Earth's remaining underground reserves of fossil fuel." This is

---

[21] The researchers were led by James Hansen, the director of NASA's Goddard Institute for Space Studies, and the first scientist to warn the U.S. Congress of global warming. The others were Makiko Sato, Pushker Kharecha, Gary Russell, David Lea and Mark Siddall. This figure (of "10 years") and this paper may well have inspired the 4-hour CNN program, *Planet in Peril* (aired Oct. 23/24, 2007), which in turn inspired our VP Ted Stalets to create www.PlanetinPeril.org.

not even *imaginable* to most people, and it must truly terrify those who run or own shares in big oil companies.[22]

The problem, as described by Stephen Lewis,[23] is that while the issue has finally caught on, "Very few governments [are] taking it seriously."[24] He then elaborated: "Climate change almost moves beyond the scale of human understanding.... We're shadowing the possibility of an apocalypse in the latter half of this century, and that has not been fully grasped—certainly not by the policy makers.... After the year 2050, this world is in terrible trouble unless we come to our senses now.... We are almost beyond the point of human intervention.... [It seems that] we don't give a damn about future generations.... [Humanity] is on the brink of a catastrophe unlike any other ... and ... there has to be an emergency response."

Is Stephen Lewis a "shrill alarmist"? He certainly is not.

> **We appeal, as human beings to human beings: Remember your humanity and forget the rest. If you can do so, the way lies open to a new Paradise; if you cannot, there lies before you the risk of universal death.** Albert Einstein (in his last signed public statement)

Just days before this book was submitted to the publisher, the IPCC issued (from Valencia, Spain) its fourth report in this calendar year. It was November 16, 2007, and MSNBC ran a piece[25] under the banner headline, "U.N. issues landmark report on global warming." A subordinate headline reads: "Panel offers dire warnings, establishes scientific baseline for political talks." The IPCC delegates declared the debate about the science of climate change to be over, and warned that as a result of human activity, the Earth is hurtling toward a warmer age at a quickening pace. UN Secretary-General Ban Ki-moon said climate change imperils "the most precious treasures of our planet," and that the potential impact of global warming is "so severe and so sweeping that only urgent, global action will do." The MSNBC piece, quoting the IPCC report, said that unless action is taken very soon,

---

[22] I trust you realize I am being ironic. At this time, oil companies aren't the least bit worried about this, because they know ... or at least they *think* they know ... that human beings will *never* stop burning oil and gas, not even if it costs them ... well, everything, actually ... their world, their future ... their own children's lives and futures. Either we leave all the fossil fuels in the ground or we commit omnicide. Make a decision. Or ... am I just being ironic again?

[23] Canada's former UN Special Envoy for HIV and AIDS in Africa; he is now Professor in Global Health, Faculty of Social Sciences at McMaster University. He was responding to questions from Jay Ingram, host of *Daily Planet*, on the Discovery Channel, in 2007.

[24] The single exception, in his judgement, is the government of the UK.

[25] http://www.msnbc.msn.com/id/21844627/

human activity could lead to "abrupt and irreversible changes ... *that would make the planet unrecognizable.*" (Emphasis added.)

Ban Ki-moon called climate change "the defining challenge of our age," and he is right. I am quite astonished to see the right words finally being spoken, but as Stephen Lewis said above, the policy-makers in governments still aren't taking the actions that are clearly required to save our lives, our children's lives and our world. Next (in December, 2007) comes an IPCC gathering in Indonesia, and that is where policy makers will either cope or not cope. We must surely hope that they come to their senses and build on the Kyoto Protocol, but my experience tells me that it won't likely happen, and that we will never get this "crisis" under control unless we also build a democratic world government.

> **Our technical civilization has just reached its greatest level of savagery. We will have to choose, in the more or less near future, between collective suicide and the intelligent use of our scientific conquests.... Before the terrifying prospects now available to humanity, we see even more clearly that peace is the only goal worth struggling for. This is no longer a prayer but a demand to be made by all peoples to their governments, a demand to choose definitively between hell and reason.** Albert Camus, French resistance newspaper *Combat*, August 8, 1945

The newspapers are now full of reports on climate change, and on television, we find programs like *Planet in Peril* and *Can We Save Planet Earth?* TV networks don't dare to use the word "omnicide" yet, lest *they* be called shrill, I suppose, but they have at least correctly identified the issue as the looming end of civilization or our species, brought on by our own activities. So the question arises: What can you and I *really* do, beyond using a bit less gas by switching to car-sharing[26] or using our votes to elect the "greenest" candidates in an election? Should we tune the issue out and just have a good time, as many people seem to be doing? Should we just pay our taxes and leave it to government officials or scientists to find a solution, as we do for so many other problems? Here is my answer, in story form.

You pull off the highway for gas. A mechanic investigates a disturbing sound coming from your car. He tells you part of the steering mechanism is malfunctioning, and if you don't get it fixed, you may crash and die. He

---

[26] Cars are parked strategically around a city and are then used by several people on an hourly rate ($3 to $10/hour). The car users book time via the Internet, and it saves them money and pollutes less since you only use a car when you must. And when you don't use the car, you pay nothing. Look into it.

demands your car keys, explaining that he may be legally or morally liable if he lets you drive away. In an analogous situation, a bartender doesn't allow a drunken customer to drive away from his bar.

These are examples of responsible interventions. Whether their actions are grounded in morality or law, these "interveners" acted to safeguard the welfare of other drivers, passengers or pedestrians who could also suffer if the drunk and the driver of the unsafe car had been allowed to just continue on their merry way.

Similarly, if humanity is now committing omnicide, it behoves everyone with a brain, a heart or a soul to scream: "Stop, you fools—you'll kill us all!" In other words, what is needed today is not one more scholarly study, but some solid traction on the ground in the form of a bona fide *strategy* that gets us off the current trajectory towards oblivion, and onto a much more reasonable path, one that leads to a sustainable future.

> **If men can develop weapons that are so terrifying as to make the thought of global war include almost a sentence for suicide, you would think that man's intelligence and his comprehension ... would include also his ability to find a peaceful solution.** U.S. President Dwight D. Eisenhower, Press Conference, Washington, DC, November 14, 1956

> **I want to save the world, but I don't know how.** Céline Dion,[27] singer, in a CBC interview with Evan Solomon, Sunday, November 19, 2006

I call for such an intervention, *by you*, into the activities of the human species.[28] We must identify the individuals and institutions that are behind these unacceptable risks or unsustainable activities, and somehow limit their power to control the direction that our civilization is traveling in. The only conceivable way to do that is to construct a new centre of political gravity, a

---

[27] These words were in response to a question about what she planned to do after her incredibly successful five-year run in Las Vegas. Dion went on to say that if the experts were in charge of things, whatever they were doing wasn't working very well, and maybe it was time to ask mothers what we should do to save the world. (She and her husband have a young son that they adore.)

[28] On your own behalf, on behalf of your progeny, on behalf of all humanity, but also on behalf of the countless species that cannot communicate using a human language, and hence have no voice in this conversation. (If animals could vote in the global referendum, they would vote 100% "yes" to the proposition that humans govern themselves globally and stop threatening life on Earth.)

new trustee of people-power that is truly global in scope but, unlike the UN, is directly elected, and democratic—an institution that is accountable to the people of planet Earth, and not to national governments.

> **What's happening** [referring to the IPCC report] **is that the scientists, who are the most cautious people on the planet, have now said that we have less than ten years** [!] **to slow global warming down or else … we have a crisis, we've been warned about this for two decades now, and no one is paying attention.** Laurie David in an HBO interview (April 22, 2006). She produced *An Inconvenient Truth*, the Oscar-winning documentary on global warming that starred Al Gore.

> **The earth is not dying, it is being killed. And the people who are killing it have names and addresses.** Utah Phillips, singer, storyteller, archivist, historian, activist, philosopher, radio show host

As you should be able to conclude from these first pages, our situation has been called dire, and it *is* dire, but it appears that most people have no sense of the magnitude or the imminence of the threat, and so they live in a collective state of denial. You may even *be* one of these "in denial" people. Although the likelihood of our fixing all that we have made wrong with the world may not be great, you have two obvious options. You can say that we have ruined the planet and just accept that there is nothing you can do, or you can muster the strength and courage—the guts, if you will—to repair things. And that brings us to the question of what we *should* do, *exactly*, not only to repair the damage done, but also to prevent *future* human actions from *ever again* endangering life on Earth.

> **While we must be prepared to meet the trial if war comes, we should gear foreign and domestic policies toward the ultimate goal, the abolition of war from the face of the earth. You cannot control war; you can only abolish it.** In #6 of Rotary's "Seven Paths to Peace"

> **I am a patriot of humanity. I am a citizen of the world.** Charlie Chaplin [French original: Je suis un patriote de l'humanité. Je suis un citoyen du monde.]

> **It is my opinion that the safety of the world, its protection against the unimaginable devastation of an atomic war, depends upon the institution of a democratic world-wide government — a government of the people themselves…. The experience of generation after generation has shown that pacts and treaties between nations do not avert war, but lead to war. Only a democratic union of the people provides safety and peace.** Linus Pauling, Nobel Laureate

Please answer this key question. If you could do something that has a real chance of saving the planet from human abuse—now and forever—something that is legal and easy and would take up only a few hours of your time in the next few weeks, would you do it? If you just said or thought "yes," you may want to jump ahead to Chapter 13 and get cracking on your assignment *while* you read the rest of the book. Or you can just read on and deal with this specific, personal challenge when you reach Chapter 13 the old-fashioned way.

> **There's been a quantum leap technologically in our age, but unless there's another quantum leap in human relations, unless we learn to live in a new way towards one another, there will be a catastrophe.**
> Albert Einstein

> **Nations that prepare for war usually get what they prepare for.** Albert Einstein

> **Today I can declare my hope and declare it from the bottom of my heart that we will eventually see the time when that number of nuclear weapons is down to zero and the world is a much better place.** General Colin Powell, U.S. Army, then chair of U.S. Joint Chiefs of Staff, June 10, 1993, at Harvard University

> **We must inoculate our children against militarism, by educating them in the spirit of pacifism … Our schoolbooks glorify war and conceal its horrors. They indoctrinate children with hatred. I would teach peace rather than war, love rather than hate.** Albert Einstein

Chapter 2

The fix

> **There is no salvation for civilization, or even the human race, other than the creation of a world government.** Albert Einstein

There are many books outlining the terrible mess we have made of this world, and a few explain how a democratic world government would likely work, if only we had one (see the bibliography). The books that do address democratic world government look mostly at the structure, economics and responsibilities of the proposed world body, and as the possibility of global governance grows, other scholarly works will inevitably emerge. This book is not meant to break very much new ground in those areas. It is basically a plan to compel the creation of such a global institution. It presents a new and powerful political instrument, the global referendum, as the necessary tool that we, the people of the Earth, could use to achieve a democratically governed world in as little as a decade, all (I trust) without firing a shot.

> **You cannot separate the means from the end because the means are the end in process.** Martin Luther King, Jr. (paraphrased)

If we are to create a truly democratic world government (the acronym is "DWG"), the first thing we need to face is the fact that *national governments will never do it* (at least not on their own; not in the absence of a powerful worldwide demand from the grassroots). If they had wanted to, they would have done it already. However, this failure by our nation states is no reason to assume that this job can't be done. In the past, "people-power" has compelled dramatic political changes in spite of what national governments wanted or said or did. If we, the people of the world, make our demand heard and convert this goal into a real possibility, national governments will quickly research this idea, and conclude that democratic world government would be a very positive development for them too.[29] Business leaders

---

[29] In fact the only national government that could find it to be a disadvantage is the one nation that currently acts as if it were the world's policeman, the USA. No one elected the USA to such a role, and in any event, most people think that the USA is doing a terrible job of it anyway. In a few years, those in favour of a democratic world government will likely

know that political instability is very bad for business; and their self-interest "instinct" will kick in when and as they realize that political stability and sustainable global economic conditions can best be achieved or maintained by a democratic world government. *Even terrorists* should see the DWG as a positive step, in that they would have a new planetary forum in which to air their grievances, a new global legal order in which all *legitimate* grievances should and must be effectively redressed.[30]

> **I like to believe that people in the long run are going to do more to promote peace than our governments. I think that people want peace so much that one of these days [national] governments had better get out of the way and let them have it.** Dwight D. Eisenhower

The task at hand is to find a way to *peacefully* mobilize global public opinion to such an extent as to achieve our stated goal. Compelling the establishment of a DWG will require the activation of people-power on a scale that has never before been seen, the global scale, and the weight and force of this unprecedented mobilization must be brought to bear on all national governments and on every other entity that argues for business as usual. When it dawns on all people that our species has been "committing omnicide"[31] for many decades, at that sad-but-hopeful moment, we will all know what we have to do. We are, in a sense, "on our own," and we must be up to the challenge as individual human beings.

> **I would rather have peace in the world than be President.** Former U.S. president Harry S. Truman

I would compare this event to the period in 2000 when my wife and I became the full-time guardians of her two kids. Their father hadn't smoked for fifteen years, but he died of lung cancer. I was a very heavy smoker back then, and while I'd tried unsuccessfully to quit dozens of times, now I just

---

include a great majority of people, all or most religions, plus most national, provincial and municipal governments—a coalition of forces that cannot be denied, I would think.

[30] It is time that we discredited the view that Islamic extremists "hate freedom," as President Bush has so often insisted. Indeed, insofar as the recruitment of young suicide bombers by terrorist organizations is growing fast, it is time we looked at the real possibility that the establishment of a DWG is perhaps the *only* way to stop the so-called war on terror in a just and satisfactory manner.

[31] As in "committing suicide," except that to commit omnicide, we would have to kill pretty much *everybody*.

had to quit, or I would never make it as a stepfather. I managed to do it, but it was *very* difficult. Similarly, the human race now *has no choice* but to quit the several planet-destroying bad habits that we are addicted to. It will be very hard to slash our production of greenhouse gases and not make war *at all*, but we must do both these things, and more, if we are to survive.

> **We have been engaged in a civil war of humanity for millennia. We have … killed each other over religion, tribe, ethnicity and nationality. In all these battles we allow our secondary identities, our national identity, our religious identity, our tribal identity and others to overcome our primary identity, our human identity. In short we lose our humanity. Our existing political systems have blinded us to our humanity by imprisoning us in a conceptual paradigm in which only national political goals are imaginable.** From Lyndon Storey's summary of his book, *Humanity or Sovereignty*

To do all of these things, we will have to learn to think outside the box, reclaim our imaginations, review the hard lessons of history, screw up our courage and bring the full weight of humanity's demands to bear on anyone who refuses to accept the fundamental changes that are required of us to assure the indefinite survival of our species, and of all life on Earth. And we will have to do all of this in a way that is non-violent. Violence is one of our main "addictions," and a major element of the human problem, so it cannot be *any* part of the solution.[32]

In his famous 1961 farewell speech, former U.S. president Dwight D. Eisenhower warned the people of America and the world to beware of "unwarranted" power in the hands of what he had termed the "military-industrial complex."[33] That was most excellent advice, but it was advice that humanity didn't heed at the time, and has not heeded since (mostly, I think, because we just didn't know how).

> **My first wish is to see this plague of mankind, war, banished from the earth.** George Washington

---

[32] Except in a situation where force might be required for policing purposes, to enforce world law on behalf of humankind, once the DWG is in place—just as local police sometimes need to use force to keep the peace in a neighbourhood, even in the best democratic countries.

[33] The full quotation is: "In the councils of government, we must guard against the acquisition of unwarranted influence, whether sought or unsought, by the military-industrial complex. The potential for the disastrous rise of misplaced power exists and will persist."

Let's be very clear about this. If we are ever going to eliminate violence from the human agenda, we will have to rein in the people who are trained and paid to do violence "for" us (the military), and those who profit from war (large corporations and arms dealers). That is what Eisenhower implied we would have to do. It won't happen overnight, and it probably won't happen at all without a DWG to deal with the issues that we now depend on our armies and (to some extent) our multinationals to handle. The old system *is not working*, and institutionalized violence can *only* be controlled or replaced by a democratic world government.[34]

> **You never change things by fighting the existing reality. To change something, build a new model that makes the existing model obsolete.** Buckminster Fuller

Let's also be clear about our starting point. There is no popular rallying cry out there at this time demanding the prompt creation of a democratic world government. However, most people, if they are asked to think about the idea, intuitively see the sense of it, and by "most people," I mean about 75%. These are first reactions, and there are many serious questions still to be addressed,[35] but we have to start somewhere, and first reactions count, especially if it's clear that we have an either-or choice. In Appendix #1, you will see that a recent multi-nation opinion poll indicated 75% (of those who expressed a view) leaning in favour of what they called a "UN parliament" (essentially meaning a DWG).

> **We can't solve problems by using the same kind of thinking we used when we created them.** Albert Einstein

---

[34] Instead of using the word "only," maybe I should have said "best," because an *undemocratic* "Big Brother"-type of world government could likely do the job too … but surely no one wants that.

[35] How would it stay in the control of the common people? How could the new institution be corruption-proofed? How can we define its mandate? Do we need a constitution for the planet first? Will a DWG have executive, legislative and judicial branches, like any *national* government? Would political parties be allowed, or are they simply impossible on the global stage, where every language, ideology, skin colour and philosophy is a minority? Which powers formerly held by the UN would better belong to the DWG? I touch on some of these in later chapters, and I refer you to the list of books in the bibliography. This book is about how we could *get* a DWG, and doesn't pretend to definitively answer all these other related questions.

> **It is a form of insanity to try to solve a problem using the same methods over and over that have not worked in the past.** David E. Christensen, *Healing the World*

One of the biggest obstacles to fundamental change is the fact that most people already have too many issues to cope with in their jobs and their families. It is difficult for most people to pay enough attention to their municipal, provincial or national politics to make informed decisions at election times. To many people, it will seem pointless to worry about solving the world's problems. However, as explained in Chapter 1, our situation has now reached a point where we have *no choice*. Each of us must form a personal attitude about these wider public concerns, and then act on it.

> **The only way to win World War III is to prevent it.** Dwight D. Eisenhower

Doing nothing or having a WWIII may be options, but they must be rejected for the sake of life, and of everything else we hold dear. National governments, individually and collectively, have shown themselves largely unable to rise above perceived self-interests in their quest for national security and unsustainable prosperity. The only serious option is for the people of the world to literally compel the creation of a democratic world government, and then make it work. That won't happen until or unless there is serious traction on the ground. But how do we get such traction? Can ordinary people have a decisive effect on the way the world is run or structured? I know it sounds impossible, or highly unlikely, but it isn't.[36]

> **There are two superpowers in the world: the United States and global opinion.** Reverend Dr. Bob Edgar, General Secretary of the U.S. National Council of Churches (in 2003)

Mona Lee and Dick Burkhart have travelled by tandem bicycle for many years, mostly in India, asking people if they want a democratic world government in which they would be politically represented as citizens of the *world* in the same basic way they are now represented as citizens of a nation,

---

[36] I know I haven't proven this point yet, but be patient. All things in good time.

a province or a city. As predicted by the poll numbers (Appendix #1), these unique champions-of-peace almost always get positive reactions from the ordinary people they speak to, most of whom have never heard anything about the possibility of creating a DWG.[37] Sadly, however, and through no one's fault, the momentum seems to stop, or evaporate, right there. At Vote World Government, we are trying to mobilize that latent support, harness it, empower it, focus it and build it into a formal global mandate.

Public opinion does everything. Dwight D. Eisenhower

I think you can be confident that there exists a solid mandate for the setting up of a DWG, a potential "yes" vote from a strong majority of the human race. Given the chance to vote and access to coherent information, we think that a majority of informed people in the global village will vote in favour of the DWG. But a mere opinion poll will not do the job, no matter what numbers emerge.

Such a global mandate must not only be proven to exist, it has to be *collected*. Even assuming we can do that, we will *still* have to find effective but non-violent ways of converting this robust public demand into reality. Also, we need to find ways to guarantee that a world government would *never* fall victim to the corruption that so frequently infects governments— including *democratic* governments—at the national, provincial and local levels, because at the global level, such corruption may well be fatal to the planet. (Fortunately, there is little doubt that we will be able to "corruption–proof" the DWG to a *very* high standard—more on this in Chapter 5.)

I am become death, shatterer of worlds. J. Robert Oppenheimer, head of the Manhattan Project, quoting the Bhagavad-Gita after the explosion of the first atomic bomb

---

If a third world war broke out in which all our nation states threw everything they had into the fray, we would wipe out the human race *and* make Earth uninhabitable for most life forms. In addition to adding the word "omnicide" to our vocabulary, we would be well advised to remember that in 2008, *we live in a world at war.* By President George W. Bush's own tally, the curiously-named "war on terror" is now actively being pursued in

---

[37] Mona has written a book about their experiences, entitled *Humbler than Dust; A Retired Couple Visits the Real India by Tandem Bicycle.*

more than 80 countries, more than one third of all nations. Does that make it a real world war?

> **What difference does it make to the dead, the orphans and the homeless, whether the mad destruction is brought under the name of totalitarianism or the holy name of liberty or democracy?** Mahatma Gandhi

In 2002, former CIA Director (1993-1995) James Woolsey said to a Washington audience: "We are in a world war ... we are in World War IV [four]." In his opinion, the Cold War was WWIII, and as a former head of the CIA, he is aware of how many millions were killed as a result of that war (and it was far from "cold" for its victims). He said that World War IV began on September 11, 2001 with the assault on the twin towers of the World Trade Center in New York.

Al-Qaeda leader Osama bin Laden has called the current war WWIII, and although we do not need to take his word for anything, he has a great influence on whether this "war on terror" keeps growing or not, and there is no indication (yet) that he or other "terrorist" leaders want to negotiate a ceasefire. (There is no precedent for ending a "war on terror," and unlike more traditional wars, supremacy of arms is unlikely to determine the final outcome *unless the USA decides to actually use its nuclear weapons, which it may do if it is losing badly.* This war is akin to a guerrilla war, and, for better or worse, history records many wins for guerrillas.)

> **So long as there are sovereign nations possessing great power, war is inevitable. That is not an attempt to say when it will come, but only that it is sure to come. That was true before the atomic bomb was made. What has been changed is the destructiveness of war.** Albert Einstein

Another thing to bear in mind is the fact that a nuclear war can erupt by accident, perhaps more easily than on purpose. We need to recognize that a small war that doesn't qualify as a "world war" but involves 1/10th of all existing nukes could be just as omnicidal as a full-blown World War III. In *Cold War Blues* (page 126), I wrote:

> The concept of "sufficiency" had literally been abandoned. In the early 1960s, General Taylor had advised President Kennedy that 100 to 200 nuclear weapons would virtually wipe out the Soviet Union.

When I asked the [Canadian] Department of National Defence about this estimate, Dr. George Lindsey confirmed it for me and told me that it was not disputed. Yet in spite of existing [at that time—the early 1980s] superpower arsenals of 50,000 nuclear warheads and double-digit global overkill capabilities, President Reagan has announced plans to build 10,000 new nuclear weapons during the 1980s.

> **We don't seem to like to think or talk much about all of this, but the hard fact is that devastation unto human extinction could be unleashed through the use—in accident, fear or anger—of any major part of our immense nuclear arsenal.** Christopher Westdal, former Canadian Ambassador to Russia

Most people know that humanity is able to nuke itself off the planet, and that we can greenhouse-gas ourselves unto actual extinction. What is not recognized is that we could also commit omnicide if a bio-weapon such as smallpox were to be used by a rogue country or a terrorist group. A smallpox[38] epidemic, even if we assume a modest "multiplier"[39] of five, would probably go global within six weeks, producing "fifty million cases … in a few months."[40] And that is with a *natural* strain of the smallpox virus. An attack using a vaccine-resistant or "weaponized" strain (which is reportedly easy to make if you have a sample of the natural virus) *could* well result in omnicide. There are many other readily available bio-weapons (anthrax, the *E. coli* bacterium, botulism) for a terrorist to use. And attacks on the American food supply (and that of its allies) by al-Qaeda are now considered likely, according to security experts.

---

[38] Both the USA and Russia (the former Soviet Union) have frozen stocks of smallpox, a terrible disease that the UN cleared from the natural environment decades ago. According to Richard Preston, in *The Demon in the Freezer*, there is reason to worry that some seed samples may have been stolen or weaponized (or both). It should be noted that the U.S. military immunizes its soldiers against smallpox—*even though there is no smallpox whatsoever in the natural environment!*

[39] Used in mathematical modeling, an "R-zero" is the estimate of the number of secondary cases that will probably be caused by one infectious case before the infected person can be located, diagnosed and quarantined. Known technically as R-zero, it can be referred to more simply as the "multiplier" of the disease.

[40] Richard Preston, *The Demon in the Freezer*, page 48. Fifty million deaths is a guesstimate by Preston, and although this is not omnicide, it would be a major disaster. And we would do well to recall that the anthrax deaths after 9/11 were never solved, meaning that the perpetrators of any large-scale bio-attack may remain unknown while tens of millions of innocent people gradually perish.

> **A full scale nuclear exchange, lasting less than 60 minutes ... could wipe out more than 300 million Americans, Europeans, and Russians, as well as untold numbers elsewhere. And the survivors--as Chairman Khrushchev warned the Communist Chinese, "the survivors would envy the dead." For they would inherit a world so devastated by explosions and poison and fire that today we cannot conceive of its horrors.** John F. Kennedy, on the *Limited Test Ban Treaty*, July, 1963

Surely everyone knows well that suicide doesn't constitute any kind of a defence. There are many sound, solid reasons to create a democratic world government besides the permanent prevention of all war,[41] but the single item that changes this goal from a good idea into an urgent necessity is this new level of destruction that comes along with modern warfare, this new *consequence-of-war*, the aspect of omnicide, which exists only because of our big human brains, or rather because of technology, which is, in its turn, the product of our big human brains.

Let's imagine it's about 500,000 BCE.[42] If a male hominid ran amok psychologically, and tried to kill all of his group-mates, he might be able to break a few bones before the others could overpower him (and probably kill him, as a punishment *and* as a deterrent to others). Now, hike forward in your mind to 50,000 BCE, and add an axe to the picture. This harm-doer might kill a dozen hominids before he is subdued or killed. Next, imagine it is the 19th century, and toss a box of dynamite into the mix.[43] There may be hundreds or thousands of dead before this "criminal" or "madman" could be stopped. And finally, fast-forward to today, throw in a backpack nuke or a biological agent, and one "terrorist" can trigger a nuclear holocaust or a global pandemic.

> **Unless we establish some form of world government, it will not be possible for us to avert a World War III in the future.** Former UK prime minister Winston Churchill

---

[41] We are rapidly polluting ourselves unto extinction, for instance, and it is impossible to find the trillions of dollars needed to clean up that mess when those trillions of dollars are being used to pay, feed and equip soldiers.

[42] For those who haven't heard, the acronym "BCE" means "before the common era," and it is the modern term for "BC." What used to be called "AD" is now "CE," which means "of the common era."

[43] Alfred Nobel, the inventor of dynamite and creator of the Nobel Prizes, was of the opinion that the horror of using his explosive substance as a weapon would be so great that it would bring an end to war itself. He was a good inventor and a good man, but not a very good prophet.

As former British prime minister Margaret Thatcher once expressed it in describing her situation in terms of defending against terrorist attacks by the IRA: "We have to be right every time, and they only have to be right once."[44] With the assistance of our technology, the *offence* in any physical conflict is at such a tremendous advantage that it can generally *overwhelm the defence*.[45] Even the half-century-old doctrine of "mutual assured destruction" that secured the so-called balance of power (or balance of terror) between the USA and the former Soviet Union during the Cold War was based on the critical assumption that both sides had the ability to wipe the other side out many times over with their *offensive* weapons, but neither side had the faintest smidgen of a hope of actually *"defending"* itself against the other side's missiles. Former U.S. senator George Mitchell (the architect of the *Mitchell Plan for Middle East Peace*) perhaps described our infuriating dilemma best when he said:[46]

> We benefit enormously from technology every day of our lives ... but we also suffer from the consequences of technology.... It is now easier, takes fewer people, less skill, [and] fewer resources to kill large numbers of people than at any time in human history, and so ... a smaller and smaller minority can have a decisive adverse effect.

We cannot ban science or technology, nor should we even want to, but if these potent products of human ingenuity threaten to do more harm than good, we must either control them or accept that we are going to destroy ourselves.[47] Since *knowingly* committing omnicide is just unacceptable to all reasonable people, we must ensure that it *never* happens, either deliberately or accidentally, not even with the unimaginably powerful technologies that will surely exist in a million *years* or a million *generations* (if humanity survives so long—and it would be nice to think that we will).

With regard to the danger that we pose to ourselves, we have to assume that it is not too late to launch a program to fix all that has gone wrong with

---

[44] This famous observation is often repeated by security experts whenever terrorism is in the conversation, even if it is nothing but an illuminating glimpse of the obvious.

[45] The USA had no problem "taking" Iraq quickly in 2003, but once it was there, the tactics of the insurgency have now (mid-2007) put the USA on the defence, where they are losing, just as the "most powerful nation in the world" lost in Vietnam. The dilemma, as is often said in the American media, is that there are no "big ideas" lying around out there other than the "cut and run" option (which they euphemistically refer to as "redeployment") for the USA. The truth is, there is one big idea that would do the job, *democratic world government*, but national governments are not even considering it ... most unfortunately.

[46] From a TV interview with Aaron Brown on CNN, May 9, 2002.

[47] There is no "preordained destiny" for human society. We have serious choices to make, and we will either make them or fail to make them.

our advanced civilization. But we must heed Tim Flannery's warning (in his book, *The Weather Makers*) that if we don't change course in the very near future, "it will be too late for a reversal."[48] We need to turn our full attention to this problem immediately, and when it comes to deciding what to do about it, it would be prudent for us to assume we will have one chance, and one chance only, to get it right.[49]

> **Henceforth, every nation's foreign policy must be judged at every point by one consideration: does it lead us to a world of law and order or does it lead us back to anarchy and death?** Albert Einstein

We have arrived at a moment in history when humanity must choose between cooperation and death, and no rational person would knowingly choose death, especially if an alternative was available and achievable. In political terms, the choice is between the rule of law and the law of the jungle, meaning the "might is right" school of thought (or no law at all). More precisely, the choice we have is between a governed world and a global free-for-all, where victory usually goes to the meanest, the biggest or the sneakiest. In calmer language, we have to choose between government and anarchy.

> **We have before us the opportunity to forge for ourselves and for future generations a new world order—a world where the rule of law, not the law of the jungle, governs the conduct of nations.** President George Herbert Walker Bush in 1991

Within our nations, all people want and need security, not just because no one wants to die arbitrarily, but also so that we can do all those things

---

[48] Tim Flannery's book warns of the threat of climate change, caused by us humans and leading to our species' demise in a few generations unless dramatic action is taken *immediately*. Yet few people realize the trouble we are in, and for several decades, we have had "climate change deniers," who are much like Holocaust deniers in that they are just not willing to let scientific facts stand in the way of a perfectly good belief. On February 2, 2007, the UN's Intergovernmental Panel on Climate Change released its final report, in which the world's leading climate scientists concluded that global warming is mostly the result of human-produced greenhouse gases. And then they said, in effect, "We've done our job, and now it is up to the policy-makers."

[49] It is also prudent to realize that no national government can fix what ails us, and that the UN couldn't even get Rwanda fixed, never mind a crash of the entire world's civilization. It is also prudent to conclude that time is short to put a democratic world government in place to try to repair "spaceship Earth."

that make life worth living—raise a family, acquire knowledge, work, play, travel, enjoy the world—things that cannot be done well or done at all if some people run around killing other people with guns or blowing things up—or blowing themselves up, for that matter. There is only one reliable, proven way to minimize violence *within* a nation, and that is law (law *with justice*, of course).

> **The world no longer has a choice between force and law; if civilization is to survive, it must choose the rule of law.** Dwight D. Eisenhower

To make and enforce law requires an effective government. In most areas, people have chosen, or at least accepted, "governance" over anarchy, with near-unanimity, and I have no doubt that people will continue to make that choice *within* all nations. The need for law (including an independent judiciary and responsive government) is sure to increase as the power of our technology increases. Most people know very well that for law to work, law enforcement, though necessary at times, is only part of the equation. The foundation of law rests on its acceptance by the majority of people, and a general recognition that any weaknesses in the law can be addressed and must be addressed within the political arena.

> **We must create worldwide law and law enforcement as we outlaw worldwide war and weapons.** John F. Kennedy

Even in the 21st century, in this age of overkill weaponry, every national government is expected to provide security to its people against all external threats, including military attacks from nuclear-armed foreign countries and global threats such as climate change or pandemics. Although there are no effective military responses to most of these threats, national governments are simply not ready to implement institutional responses, like world law.[50]

There appear to be no alternative options on the *planetary* level than the one that we tried *and had success with* at the national level. A GlobeScan poll (Appendix #1), conducted in 2004, is good evidence that most people now

---

[50] In fairness, however, during the latter part of the twentieth century, national governments significantly expanded the body of international law, articulated numerous fundamental legal principles and recognized significant inalienable rights of individuals, so there is now a widely recognized written foundation on which to build. What is lacking is a widespread willingness by governments to abide by all those fine words, and a credible system of enforcement.

support the establishment of a democratic world government (or "UN parliament," as the poll described it) to create and enforce a body of world law.[51] An average of 63% of all the respondents from 18 nations were in favour, while only 20% were opposed (17% neither favoured it nor opposed it, or they answered "don't know," or gave no answer). That's more than three to one in favour (75%+) among those who expressed an opinion.

> **It will be just as easy for nations to get along in a republic of the world as it is for you to get along in the republic of the United States. Now when Kansas and Colorado have a quarrel over the water in the Arkansas River, they don't call out the National Guard in each state and go to war over it. They bring suit in the Supreme Court of the United States and abide by the decision. There isn't a reason in the world why we can't do that internationally.** Harry S. Truman, June 28, 1945, on receiving an honorary degree from the University of Kansas City

There is every reason to believe and expect that people can live within *world* law as comfortably as they now live within national or provincial or municipal law. Once we have world law, any suggestion that we abandon it will seem as ridiculous as the suggestion today that we do away with these other levels or layers of law.

> **The only way peace can be achieved is through world government.**
> Jawaharlal Nehru, 1st prime minister of the Republic of India

Although law is often maddeningly slow to change, it is not intended to just maintain the status quo. It is meant to evolve non-violently, and it is the *proven* way of managing human relations without violence. Law is the means by which we avoid pitched battles between and among neighbours or cities or provinces. Adults in any democratic society are expected to be able to resolve all their disputes without violence, and if informal negotiations do not work, our system of law is the final arbiter. We must learn to manage *all* differences, *including those between and among nation states*, without violence, and especially without the reality of war or even the threat of war. It will require a lot of work to resolve every serious dispute peacefully, but we have to do

---

[51] This is not the same as international law. World law, like national, provincial and municipal law, applies (*inter alia*) to individuals. International law amounts to treaties, applies to the *governments of nations*, and is largely unenforceable. (Well, it is more complicated than this, but that's the essential difference.)

that ... starting now, and lasting forever into the future. This is not just a tough choice that we are well advised to make; this is now a condition of our survival, of our continued existence on Earth, a new "rule" that arrived on our agenda uninvited, and did so as a direct result of the power of our technologies.

Whenever people have been allowed to decide the *kind* of government they wanted, they have invariably decided on a form of democracy.[52] Any dictator can make law and enforce it through fear,[53] but this doesn't lead to security or justice, and often results in violence or in revolution. While there are many variations on the general theme of democracy, I would suggest that any national population, given an informed and *free* choice, will choose to have democracy of one sort or another.

As Alfred Emanuel Smith said: "All the ills of democracy can be cured by more democracy."[54] And as Reinhold Niebuhr[55] said: "Man's capacity for justice makes democracy possible, but man's inclination to injustice makes democracy necessary."

Peace requires Justice; Justice requires Law; Law requires Government, not only within Nations, but equally between Nations.
William Penn, American Quaker, political theorist, 1693

To create a world government, there are many particulars to be worked out, and the dilemma is *how* to decide those details. Some of the problems involved are unique, without parallel or precedent in history. And even if we can make comparisons with the history of one country, we have to remember that most democracies used to be far less democratic than they are today. Some evolved from monarchies, some grew from colonial status,

---

[52] There may be some principalities, kingdoms or tribal areas where this is not the case, but then oppressed people do not always realize they are oppressed, and a truly fair referendum in these areas would likely produce a good mandate for democratic governance. One thing is certain; the population of any democratic nation would *never* vote to discard democracy in favour of an autocratic system of governance (except in the very rare circumstance where a government asks for and gets popular support for *temporarily* suspending civil rights due to a war or insurrection).

[53] It can get quite involved to debate which form of authoritarian or totalitarian rule is worse than which others, or whether any system can be completely free of arbitrary or unfair (or downright stupid) decisions. This is not a discussion I will pursue in this book.

[54] Winston Churchill once quipped that the best argument *against* democracy is a five-minute chat with the average voter. But he also told the British Parliament that: "Democracy is the worst form of government except all those other forms that have been tried." (This is often misquoted as "... except for the alternatives.")

[55] Protestant theologian known for relating the Christian faith to modern politics and diplomacy. He is a crucial contributor to modern "just war" thinking.

or were created only after the violent overthrow of a dictator or of a class that had held all the power and most of the wealth to itself. No violent process will work at the global level; not in a world filled with weapons of mass destruction. We must create a world government *quickly*, and we must do it *right*, meaning non-violently and democratically.

I'm very supportive of what you are putting together ... I wish you the best ... keep me posted. Walter Cronkite (message left on my answering machine October 5, 2004, in response to my inquiry)

There is also the very difficult question of who or what decides these particulars. If one argues that it takes a world government to decide how a world government has to be structured or empowered, then there will never be a world government. Circular reasoning doesn't help us, and can easily be defeated. If this kind of reasoning had merit, we could argue that all laws would have to be spelled out in advance before anyone could really decide whether to support the general notion of law. Democratically decided laws are many centuries old in some nations, and those nations are still making a lot of new laws at all three levels of government,[56] as society evolves. The argument that we must write and agree upon a constitution for a governed world *before* doing anything else is not tenable.[57] A written constitution for the world is a terrific idea, a necessary idea, and one that must be completed at some point (and then ratified by means of a *second* global referendum, at a future date), but please ... first things first. Job #1 is to secure the approval and "authorization" of the human race for the *establishment* of the DWG. (I want Canada to finance a global convention to draft a world constitution, by the way, because it needs to be done, and because our country can afford to pay the expenses of such a global gathering—see Chapter 12.)

---

[56] I realize that not all places have a provincial (or state) level of government in between the municipal and the national levels, but most do.

[57] The World Constitution and Parliament Association has been working on such a constitution for many decades, but few people are even aware of its existence. The document they have produced may be a wonderful constitution, or not, but it is of little value unless there is first a demand for a world government. And once that exists, it will be necessary to start from scratch, with individuals, NGOs, scholars, governments and others involved in the framing process. I am not qualified to assess the document the WCPA has produced. Their "strategy" was to finish the document and then get national governments to sign on, one at a time. So far no national government has signed on. Our approach is to start with the people, and then see if national governments want to support us. As stated elsewhere, the electors of a DWG are not national governments, but the people—the human race. If the electors are the national governments, we'll end up with another UN-type body, which is *not* what is needed.

> **Government is the thing. Law is the thing. Not brotherhood, not international cooperation, not security councils that can only stop war by waging it.... Where does security lie anyway -- security against the thief, the murderer? In brotherly love? Not at all. It lies in government.**
> E.B. White, former editor of *The New Yorker* magazine and the author of *Charlotte's Web*

The argument for starting with a comprehensive constitution is that without one, we would be asking all people to buy "a pig in a poke."[58] The problem is that we now have a choice between a pig in a poke and no pig at all. This analogy only goes so far. A pig is a pig, and the elements necessary for a democratic government are reasonably well settled. We know what a democratic government is even before the details of a new one have been worked out.

There are certain principles that must be accepted as essential, such as the equality of all people before the law, or defined limits on the mandate of the DWG, and of course democratically elected representatives. But we do not need to sort out every detail before asking people to support the general goal as defined on the referendum ballot. And while the global mandate is under construction, the work on a draft constitution can begin.[59]

> **The founders** [of the United Nations] **sought to replace a world at war with a world of civilized order. They hoped that a world of relentless conflict would give way to a new era, one where freedom from violence prevailed.... But the awful truth is that the use of violence for political gain has become more, not less, widespread in the last decade.** Former U.S. president Ronald Reagan to the UN General Assembly, September 26, 1983

It should also be remembered that there are quite a large number of documents (such as the *Universal Declaration of Human Rights*) and other principles that have been developed by the United Nations, and these can be adopted entirely or in part by the DWG (some perhaps as elements of

---

[58] The "poke" in this expression refers to a bag or sack, and the expression "don't buy a pig in a poke" means you should not buy anything unless you can see it first.

[59] I would hope that by the time the global referendum authorizing the creation of the DWG is finished, a draft constitution would be essentially ready, but we may be disappointed in this regard. The application of corruption-proofing and "total transparency" procedures (as outlined in Chapter 5) to the constitutional drafting process is one way of helping the drafters to get past red herrings and phoney obstructions. More on this later, in Chapter 12.

the proposed world constitution, others in some other manner). Such documents or principles would surely stand a much better chance of being implemented under the DWG than they did when they were the product of the UN, since a DWG is not subject to any vetoes by the Security Council, and can't be second-guessed by the national interests that often compel the delegates at the UN to vote this way or that—quite frequently against the interests of their own compatriots.

People do not make wars; governments do. Ronald Reagan

We needed the devastation of nineteen million deaths in WWI to force us to establish the League of Nations. Even then, we got it wrong, because that institution failed to prevent the recurrence of mega-death. It took the Second World War, with 38 million more deaths, to prompt us to create the United Nations ... and we got it wrong *again*. The Cold War (from the late 1940s to the late 1980s) caused about 20 million *more* deaths, even though its hot mini-wars were fought mostly by small surrogates of the (then) two superpowers and their incompatible ideologies. Unfortunately, our worthy forebears did not make the UN into a directly-elected, democratic body, and as a result, it did not become, and can surely *never* become,[60] the kind of democratic world government we need to have and to trust in if omnicide is to be forever avoided.

Our role is to promote a world organization. World citizenship is the last chance. Hervé Bazin (1911 - 1996) [Original in French: Notre rôle est de promouvoir une organisation mondiale. La citoyenneté mondiale est la dernière chance.]

We have left the peacemaking to the governments of nations—the usual combatants in wars. The UN is primarily a meeting place for nations. A review of the voting practices of most UN member states makes it clear that few (including democracies) consistently vote in ways that reflect the wishes and interests of their citizens. The UN has only a limited ability to prevent wars or deal with the injustices and cruelties that give rise to war, largely a result of the longstanding principle of non-interference in the

---

[60] There are some arguments that UN reform is possible, but any careful perusal of the UN's *Charter* would reveal that to be extremely difficult, and any basic realism tells us that the winners of WWII, who now have vetoes in the Security Council, will never willingly give up this special power.

"internal" affairs of another nation state (this is now *slowly* changing in cases where a national government doesn't or cannot provide security for its own citizens).[61] There are no UN elections or UN constituencies wherein people vote for an individual to represent them. Further, it is *most* unlikely that the UN, under its *Charter*, could compel the gradual and safe disarmament of all nations, and/or the observance by all nations (and all people) of world law. (Note: "The gradual and safe disarmament of all nations" may sound scary, wildly idealistic or perhaps addle-brained, but it does *not* imply the *complete* disarmament of all nations, any more than the creation of a nation implies any lack of required police powers or the removal of police powers from the provinces or cities within the nation.)[62]

> **We travel together, passengers on a little spaceship, dependent on its vulnerable resources of air and soil; all committed for our safety to its security and peace; preserved from annihilation only by the work, the care and, I will say, the love we give our fragile craft. We cannot maintain it half fortunate and half miserable, half confident and half despairing, half slave to the ancient enemies of man, half free in a liberation of resources undreamed of until this day. No craft, no crew, can travel safely with such contradictions. On their resolution depends the survival of us all.** Adlai Stevenson (U.S. Democrat, 1950s)

It is very hard to imagine (especially in the post-WWII climate of the late 1940s) all national governments giving up the amount of sovereignty that would have to be surrendered for such a sensitive power transition.[63] Of course back then it was not yet realized that a WWIII or auto exhaust emissions could be omnicidal, and that is what makes the situation today so different. One way or another, we have to abandon any hope that the UN is going to evolve into the kind of democratic world government we need—at least not in time to prevent WWIII and not in time to deal effectively with climate change.

---

[61] A so-called "duty to protect" has been supported by many NGOs, and is now adopted "in principle" by the UN General Assembly, but being thus adopted in the past has often meant little or nothing in terms of the actual authorization of interventionist activities designed to protect the victims of cruelties, especially if the "criminal" is a national government (witness the ongoing Darfur genocide).

[62] The UN has been working on disarmament since UNSSOD 1 (the UN Special Session on Disarmament), in 1978, without making much progress on the issue.

[63] It should not be conceded that this (a surrender of some sovereignty) is what was actually required, but that is the way it would have been perceived, and was perceived, back then—as the "surrender of some amount of sovereignty" (and hence some freedom) *by* nation states *to* a supranational body. More on this later.

> **The world does not suffer from lack of finance for the UN but from lack of government, and from lack of appreciation for the fact which Boutros Boutros-Ghali pointed out to President Clinton: The UN is not, and never could become, a global government.** Harold S. Bidmead, *Tilting at Windbags: The Autobiography of a World Federalist* (NOTE: The so-called windbags are the United Nations and its apologists or boosters.)

Several modest structural reforms, like enlarging the non-veto-bearing membership of the Security Council, were proposed in a UN report to then-Secretary-General Kofi Annan in December of 2004, but even these seem very unlikely to ever be implemented.[64] The refusal of all the nuclear powers who signed the *Non-Proliferation Treaty* (NPT) in 1970 to "… pursue negotiations in good faith on effective measures relating … to nuclear disarmament, and on a treaty on general and complete disarmament (or GCD) under strict and effective international control" (Article VI), *as they agreed to do*, should leave little doubt on this point. Their failure to disarm— *or even keep their word regarding negotiations*—has resulted in an ever-expanding nuclear "club," ever-decreasing national security and world security and an ever-increasing danger of omnicide.

> **Democratic World Government is the only imaginable positive future for humanity.** Timothy Roscoe Carter, US lawyer, "basic income" advocate

To provide a sketch of what the democratic world government might look like and how it may function, Vote World Government has found it necessary to make several basic assumptions, based on historical precedents or on reason and common sense.

For example, we suggest that 700 DWG constituencies will be needed to include and to adequately represent all of the world's people. The world population is expected to be about seven billion in 2018 (our target year for the inaugural session of the global parliament, or DWG), so that would work out to about ten million people per DWG constituency.[65] Some U.S.

---

[64] There is a way to amend the UN *Charter* that involves a two-thirds vote in the General Assembly, but such a result is most unlikely because of the powers of persuasion of the large countries, and in any event, even if such a thing were to happen, it would not likely be ratified by the Security Council, as required.

[65] George Monbiot, the author of *The Age of Consent*, suggested there could be perhaps 600 constituencies of 10 million people each in an article he wrote for the *New Internationalist* (Jan/Feb 2002), "A parliament for the planet." That was based on the then-current human population of 6 billion or so. The same formula of 10 million per constituency leads to 700 constituencies if the world population is 7 billion, as it likely will be by 2018.

Senators now have constituencies of ten million citizens, so this is not some absurd number. The number of constituencies can of course be increased or decreased later by the DWG. This number, 700, is suggested simply as a reasonable figure, so it is possible to get things started. (Other plans for constituencies *not* based on population have been suggested, but are very unlikely to attract broad support.)

> **My country is the world, my religion is to do good, and all men are my brothers.** Thomas Paine, 18th century political philosopher

Regarding the item of how the DWG might function, we made another assumption. In the same way that national governments are well advised to stay out of the jurisdictions of provinces (or "states," in the USA) and out of the jurisdictions of cities and towns, a world government must have a *limited mandate*. Even before any first draft of its constitution is written, the architects of a DWG must understand the necessity of staying *out* of those political matters that are best left to the lower levels of government, most *especially* when it comes to matters that have traditionally been and should remain the responsibilities of national governments.

> **After all, politics is a matter of serving the community, which means that it is morality in practice. And how better to serve the community and practice morality than by seeking in the midst of the global (and globally threatened) civilization their own global political responsibility: that is, their responsibility for the very survival of the human race?** Vaclav Havel, 1st president of Czech Republic

The well-established principle of "subsidiarity" suggests that all issues should be resolved by the *smallest appropriate political unit*. I think the strictest application of this important principle will be crucial to the operation of a successful DWG.

> **What has happened to the dreams of the United Nations' founders? What has happened to the spirit which created the United Nations? The answer is clear:** [national] **governments got in the way of the dreams of the people.** Ronald Reagan, to the UN General Assembly, September, 1983

It is certainly desirable and perhaps even necessary to have national governments and all other levels of government strongly in support of the DWG. And for that to happen, we must ensure that existing governments are not unduly disturbed by what they may see as "unwelcome intrusions" into their traditional areas of competence and responsibility, just as national governments are very well advised to stay out of areas that are clearly in the jurisdictions of provinces or municipalities (even if it is not always possible). I imagine it will take a few decades to reach a point where all our national governments can fully trust, depend upon and wholeheartedly support the DWG, but clear-cut separations between their respective jurisdictions[66] will facilitate such an evolution in attitudes.

> **Though force can protect in emergency, only justice, fairness, consideration and cooperation can finally lead men** [and women] **to the dawn of eternal peace.** Dwight D. Eisenhower

Finally, although it may be necessary for our survival to have a reliable military capability at the global level, there is always the danger that it could be abused. That simply must not happen … *ever*. Although the potential misuse of military power at the global level is certainly not the only reason for conducting a super-clean political operation, it is a sufficient reason *on its own* for the permanent and full "corruption-proofing" of the DWG. Once we realize that such corruption-proofing simply *has* to be done, it is reassuring to realize that it *can* be done. (More on this in Chapter 5.)

> **True peace is not merely the absence of tension: it is the presence of justice.** Martin Luther King Jr.

I hope by now you will have come to accept (if you didn't already) that our situation really is "dire," and that the short-term and long-term *political* fix is the creation of a democratic world government. There have been non-governmental organizations promoting that goal for more than half a century, and there have been books written about it since the 1940s (see the bibliography). However, in spite of a flood of finely-crafted words and great efforts, a world government does not exist, so the question that we have to address becomes painfully obvious. How can we get it? Since our national governments will not do it, can we ordinary people authorize, empower and actually create a democratic world government?

---

[66] Eventually to be articulated in a constitution for the Earth. (See Chapter 12.)

Chapter 3

The political tool

> **The abolition of war is no longer an ethical question to be pondered solely by learned philosophers and ecclesiastics, but a hard core one for the decision of the masses whose survival is the issue.** U.S. General Douglas MacArthur, July 5, 1961

I have read many of the books that exist on the involved subject of world governance. The problem, as I see it, is that no one has yet devised a really practical plan as to how we can get ourselves from A to B, from where we are to where we need to go. No useful purpose is served by discussing the details of some theoretical world government unless we first conclude that in addition to our wish to proceed, we also possess the tools required to get the job done. Fortunately, we have the required political and technological tools.

> **A world government with powers adequate to guarantee security is not a remote ideal for the distant future. It is an urgent necessity if our civilization is to survive.** Albert Einstein

> **World government is not only possible, it is inevitable, and when it comes, it will appeal to patriotism in its truest sense, in its only sense, the patriotism of men** [and women] **who love their national heritages so deeply that they wish to preserve them in safety for the common good.** Sir Peter Ustinov, British-born actor, Goodwill Ambassador for UNICEF, president of the World Federalist Movement in 1991

As a first reaction, we expect most national governments (not all) to be loudly dismissive towards the idea of a democratic world government. We must therefore determine whether we can get the job done in the absence of their support, or maybe even in spite of their opposition. We have good reason to think we can achieve our goal no matter what governments say, primarily because we believe that a strong majority of all people will see the sense of this proposal, and demand that it be supported and carried out. At

Vote World Government, our aim (as you know from the book cover) is to conduct a global referendum to authorize (assuming it passes) the creation of a democratic world government, or "DWG."

> As in science, so it was in world politics for Einstein: he sought a unified set of principles that could create order out of anarchy. A system based on sovereign nations with their own military forces, competing ideologies and conflicting national interests would inevitably produce more wars. So he regarded a world authority as realistic rather than idealistic, as practical rather than naïve. For the remaining ten years of his life, his passion for advocating a unified governing structure for the globe would rival that for finding a unified field theory that could govern all the forces of nature. Walter Isaacson, *Einstein, His Life and Universe*, in a chapter called "One Worlder," page 488

National governments *should* respond to the idea of democratic world government favourably. With a DWG, national governments will end up with far more money for domestic programs, *and* their citizens will have far greater security, *and* this improved national security will cost less than what each country now pays for its own military defence. The current system of 194 sovereign nations requires each state to *attempt* to defend itself, and any state at war *and fearing for its life* will unquestionably use all of its weapons, including weapons of mass destruction (WMD), if it has them, even if their possession or use is prohibited under international law. And if WMD are used in an *all-out* war, we may well destroy our entire species. Humans are simply too good at war to risk war any more.

> There is only one path to peace and security: the path of supranational organization. One-sided armament on a national basis only heightens the general uncertainly and confusion without being an effective protection. Albert Einstein

If every city and town had to staff and finance its own local military establishment[67] in order to protect against all possible invasions or attacks from all neighbouring cities or towns, it is easy to see that municipal taxes would go through the roof, and the actual security of all these municipalities would be a whole lot lower. The creation of a higher-level government (in this example, a national government) that takes responsibility for security

---

[67] As was the case a few thousand years ago almost everywhere on Earth.

spares municipalities most of the cost of their own security, while increasing the actual security of municipalities.[68] With the advent of the nation, cities and towns stopped attacking each other, and thus they no longer have to worry about potential attacks from other cities or towns—a state of affairs that appears to please everyone. This same general process, carried out on the global level (the advent of a global legal order established through a democratic world government), should have an identical effect on the attitudes of national governments and on the real security of all nations (not immediately, obviously, but eventually). And as a result of this new political reality at the global level, humanity can eventually forget that it was ever a potential Earth-destroyer and become an Earth-saver … a beautiful thing, I think most people would agree.

> **Many will tell you with mockery and ridicule that the abolition of war can only be a dream—that it is the vague imagining of a visionary. But we must go on or we will go under. We must have new thoughts, new ideas, new concepts. We must break out of the straightjacket of the past. We must have sufficient imagination and courage to translate the universal wish for peace—which is rapidly becoming a necessity—into actuality.** General Douglas MacArthur

Many national governments will not recognize the significance of these new equations until later. However, there may well be a few national leaders who will quickly realize that a DWG would be very good for their national government *and* for their people, and these leaders may become the most influential allies of the human race as a whole in our quest for a sane, sensible and truly secure world. It would be desirable for us to identify and support all such national leaders at an early date in the referendum process, and if we're lucky, they will sponsor our UN resolution (Appendix #2).

> **War should belong to the tragic past, to history: it should find no place on humanity's agenda for the future.** Pope John Paul II

The first requirement for making real progress is to obtain a mandate from a majority of adult human beings. I can tell you from very personal experience (see *Cold War Blues*) that if you rely on each national government

---

[68] Meaning within the nation, and compared to what the security situation was for cities and towns before the "nation" was formed to protect all cities from all dangers, including each other.

to conduct one "segment" of the global referendum alongside their next national election, that is certainly not going to happen spontaneously. (Non-democratic governments may not have elections we can piggyback onto in any event.) Even if a few governments did that, that plan still has one fatal weakness. Every nation, no matter how small, would thereby possess what amounts to a veto—by refusing to participate, any one nation could make it impossible to complete a truly global referendum conducted this way (and I'm sure that we can all think of a few countries that would love to stall our progress towards global democracy). However, it is possible, by using the Internet, to collect the global mandate in a manner that does *not* depend on the cooperation of our national governments. In fact, it gives us a way to complete the global referendum *even in the face of opposition from all our national governments*. (More on this in Chapter 4.)

> **History is now choosing the founders of the World Federation** [he meant a form of democratic world government]. **Any person who can be among that number and fails to do so has lost the noblest opportunity of a lifetime.** Carl Van Doren, Pulitzer Prize-winning biographer

For the first time ever, the people of Earth can act politically *as a united species* … if we choose to do so. This does not mean we will all speak one language, share the same religion or blend everything we value into a kind of cultural stew—only that we can be united in our need to prevent World War III, and in our determination to create a democratic world government to ban war from the human agenda and to begin the repair of the planet's environment (among many other things). We can put the global referendum ballot "out there" electronically, and promote it for as long as it takes to reach a point where the majority of adults are factually known and *proven* to be in support of the creation of a democratic world government. And at such a time, no person, government or collection of governments would even dare to say the word "no." (Some parties might dare to *say* it, but they would have no chance of stopping our progress by that time.) We can even call this global referendum "advisory" or "non-binding" if we want, while we are in the process of doing it, but if two *billion* adults vote for something, it is a safe bet that *the thing they voted for is going to happen*.

> **There is one thing stronger than all the armies in the world, and that is an idea whose time has come.** Victor Hugo, 19th-century French author, statesman, human rights campaigner (Other translations exist.)

The effectiveness of the Internet to build a global constituency and persuade national governments has clearly been well demonstrated by the International Campaign to Ban Landmines during what is often referred to as the "Ottawa Process" (see Chapter 14). It allowed NGOs[69] around the world to bring pressure to bear on many reluctant national governments, and resulted in the finalizing and signing of the 1997 *Mine Ban Treaty* in an unprecedented short time. It stands as a fine example of what can be done if people and governments make common cause.

> **The world is dangerous not because of those who do harm, but because of those who look at it without doing anything.** Albert Einstein

There is no guarantee that even a strong global mandate will "compel" the construction of a democratic world government, even if we believe it will, but one thing *is* absolutely certain: there will never be a democratic world government *in the absence* of consent from the human population of Earth.

As the results of the global referendum on DWG roll in, and assuming an emerging robust win for the "yes" side, we will have the authority to set up a World Electoral Commission[70] to settle (for now) all disputes over the boundaries of DWG constituencies,[71] decide on the minimum voting age, on nomination eligibility, on voting methodologies and a few other practical issues. This World Electoral Commission would then have to take whatever decisions are required to allow the human race to conduct a first worldwide *general election*, where adults can vote for their official representative to the democratic world government. We at Vote World Government hope to see this first general election in 2018, and if a draft world constitution is ready by then, the human race can vote to ratify or reject it in a second global referendum, to be held in tandem with the first global general election. And by the way, it doesn't matter what we call our elected representatives, but one possibility is Member of the Global Parliament, or MGP, and I will use that one for now.

---

[69] "NGO" is the acronym for "non-governmental organization," and collectively, they (NGOs) are often referred to as "civil society."

[70] How we choose representatives to the Commission is discussed in Chapter 8.

[71] There could be as many boundary complaints as there are constituencies, or more than one complaint per constituency. Tentative solutions may have to be imposed, I think, until the actual DWG (and its judiciary) can finalize solutions. These issues may take years to resolve. Perhaps, since topography elements and religious or ethnic divides can influence the formation of electoral districts, the national governments represented at the UN could assist in the job of drawing up the most workable lines within their respective nations.

> **The concept of World Government should be looked at in a new millennium as part of a grown-up and sensible discussion.** Press release concerning Harold S. Bidmead's books, *Parliament of Man* (1992) and *Tilting at Windbags: The Autobiography of a World Federalist* (2005)

[NOTE: There is a debate in some mundialist[72] circles about the difference between a parliament and a government. In casual conversation, rightly or not, the two words are used interchangeably. The bottom line is that *a government is not democratic unless it includes an accountable parliament* (a directly-elected parliament, to put a finer point on it) and *a parliament is of little value unless it can actually govern*.]

As mentioned above, we at Vote World Government are confident that a mandate now exists in the hearts and minds of the human race for the creation of a democratic world government, and we also believe that this attitude will grow even stronger in the near future. If we are correct about this, then it is vital to recognize that the people of the world have all of the tools we need to actually *collect* that global mandate, and based upon the legitimacy of that mandate, we will empower the Electoral Commission to prepare for and manage the first global general election. Then (assuming the world constitution is ratified), the DWG will have the power to carry out its mandate, which should include the following matters as priorities:

1   Outlaw war and address its root causes;

2   Create and execute a rescue plan for the Earth's environment, and ensure a sustainable future for the planet;

3   Establish the judicial system that will be required to ensure the full observance of its laws and the resolution of disputes in areas under its jurisdiction;

4   Develop and promulgate the laws necessary to protect the rights of persons as set forth in the *Universal Declaration of Human Rights* and other globally binding instruments; and

5   Establish, train and equip a modest military peace force to ensure the full implementation of DWG policies and judicial orders in all situations where the "enforcement" of world law is clearly the only

---

[72] The word "mundialist" derives from "mundus," which is Latin for "world." It refers to organizations that emphasize world citizenship, world government, world federation, world constitution or world parliament.

way to resolve a dispute.[73] (Any use of force by the DWG must be limited to the *minimum* needed to prevail in a situation where a peaceful settlement cannot be negotiated with the government or governments involved, or where a government cannot or will not comply with its obligations under world law.)

Behind the black portent of the new atomic age lies a hope which, seized upon with faith, can work out a salvation. If we fail, then we have damned every man to be the slave of fear. Let us not deceive ourselves: we must elect world peace or world destruction. Bernard Baruch, speech to UN Atomic Energy Commission, August 14, 1946

The established political tool required for all this to happen is of course the referendum … in this instance, a global referendum. The referendum is a democratic instrument that has the full weight of history behind it. But how can we possibly hope to conduct such a global referendum if national governments won't cooperate?

To my mind, to kill in war is not a whit better than to commit ordinary murder. Albert Einstein

---

War in our time has become an anachronism. Whatever the case in the past, war in the future can serve no useful purpose. Dwight D. Eisenhower

---

Nothing that I can do will change the structure of the universe. But maybe, by raising my voice, I can help the greatest of all causes— goodwill among men and peace on earth. Albert Einstein

---

I know not with what weapons World War III will be fought, but World War IV will be fought with sticks and stones. Albert Einstein

---

[73] Especially if any nation, any religion or any ideology may once again decide that killing innocent civilians is a politically valid or a "holy" way to behave.

Chapter 4

The technological tool

> **It would be unsound fancy and self-contradictory to expect that things which have never yet been done can be done except by means which have never yet been tried.** Francis Bacon, English philosopher, statesman and essayist, best known for leading the scientific revolution

The technological tool required for ordinary people to conduct the global referendum on democratic world government is, of course, the Internet. It is very doubtful that any national government would be so self-destructive as to prevent its own citizens from using the Internet.[74] In fact, I wouldn't be surprised if the "killer app" of the Internet, the application that proves in the final analysis to be the most important and profitable of all, turns out to be its role in the achievement of world peace—by being the vehicle through which we, the people of Earth, executed the global referendum on DWG.

In 1977, I founded Operation Dismantle, a Canadian non-profit anti-nuclear-weapons organization (I served as president and CEO until 1985). Operation Dismantle sought a UN-sponsored global referendum on what we termed "balanced and verifiable nuclear disarmament."[75] Initially, most groups in the established peace movement pretty much dismissed our idea of a global referendum, but after a few years it became obvious that we had a potent new strategy that would help in the accomplishment of the goal that most peace organizations shared.[76]

The question then became whether this strategy was practical. I was challenged by the Canadian government to go to the United Nations and

---

[74] Well, there's North Korea, where there aren't even cell phones *and* there is no Internet, and perhaps a few other nations might try to block the referendum by blocking the Internet, but they'd be left out in the cold if most other national governments *didn't* interfere, and if the global referendum votes were rolling in well, and especially if some nation states became the allies of the human race in our quest to get the DWG established.

[75] Based on the concept of GCD, the so-called McCloy-Zorin Principles that had been adopted many times by the UN General Assembly (but not implemented, of course). U.S. President John F. Kennedy was in the process of negotiating a treaty with the (former) Soviet Union for the *implementation* of GCD when he was assassinated. (Of course I do not mean to suggest there is a connection between these two events.)

[76] We failed to launch that world disarmament referendum—you surely would have heard about it if we had succeeded; indeed, you surely would have *voted* in it, had we succeeded. Of course there was no Internet back then.

test the waters, and I was even given the "facilitative assistance"[77] of the Canadian Mission to the UN while I was in New York. The idea was to see if a resolution calling for such a global referendum would be supported by a goodly majority of nations in the event that it was introduced into the UN General Assembly.

> **You may say that I'm a dreamer / But I'm not the only one / I hope someday you'll join us / And the world will live as one.** John Lennon, singer-songwriter with The Beatles, from his song, "Imagine"

The plan—and the shared understanding of that time—was that if we could prove that our resolution would pass rather strongly, Canada would introduce the resolution, after which the global referendum would be done in segments, one country at a time, in conjunction with national elections (to keep costs down).[78] All this would span a decade or more. It turned out that our draft resolution had *very* broad support, and everyone conceded that it would pass strongly in the General Assembly (partly because every nation wanted to be *seen* as supporting the goal of nuclear disarmament). Sadly, when we asked the government of Canada to keep its word and propose the UN resolution, they refused—after a few months of stalling.[79] (A dozen or so nations had actually said they would *co*-sponsor our global referendum resolution *if* Canada brought it forward, but because of the Cold War politics of the day, in a world divided into spheres of influence of the two superpowers, none of our willing co-sponsors was able to act as the *primary* sponsor.)

Operation Dismantle went on to get 200+ Canadian cities and towns to actually run the nuclear disarmament referendum in conjunction with their municipal elections (for a penny or two per citizen!), but it wasn't the real thing, even if millions of Canadians got to express their opinion by voting. All of the associated debating and political activity proved very beneficial in

---

[77] I would request a meeting with an ambassador. He or she would then call the Canadian Mission to see if I was for real. The Canadian Mission would say that they would appreciate it if the ambassador could meet with me and respond to the referendum initiative, even though there was no *official* commitment by the Canadian government to propose the resolution.

[78] Non-democratic countries don't have actual elections, but dictatorships have shown that they can easily pull off a national referendum to try to "validate" the dictatorship, so they could do this *good* referendum with no difficulty *if* they were inclined to do it (or if they were pressured into it).

[79] It's a longer story than this, but it's all in *Cold War Blues*, for those who may be interested. (*Cold War Blues* is available free on the Books link at www.voteworldgovernment.org, with permission from the publisher.)

raising public awareness of the horrific dangers of nuclear war, but these referendums[80] were not only held by the wrong level of government, they were—*at best*—advisory referendums, and they had no recognized power to change anything.[81] We were totally at the mercy of governments to carry our program forward at both the international and the municipal levels, and although we had a great amount of success at the municipal level, more city and town governments in Canada chose *not* to run the ballot as compared to those who agreed to do it.[82] It was *very* frustrating, but in the early 1980s, working through official governments really was the *only* practical way we could proceed.

> **There is an increasing awareness of the need for some form of global government.** Mikhail Gorbachev, last leader of the USSR (Soviet Union)

However, this is the 21st century. Back in the early 1980s, there was no Internet available to the masses. Now, *one person in seven in the world has access to a computer linked to the Internet.*[83] This means that today, we have *a real and viable alternative* to working through all our national, provincial or municipal governments. In fact, by using the Internet, we could complete a global referendum on DWG with no cooperation from any government, with no permission slip from any government, perhaps even in the face of active opposition from many governments.

We live in a very new world, and Vote World Government intends to promote an Internet-based global referendum for as long as it takes to get the global mandate we need to win … *or* until national governments take over the *administration* of the global referendum (which would be a good thing, in my view). And this time (unlike the Operation Dismantle plan), instead of focusing on the limited goal of nuclear disarmament, the ballot

---

[80] The plural of "referendum" can be either "referendums" or "referenda." While both are right, those who say "referendums" think the other pronunciation is snobby, as if to brag that one has studied Latin. Those who say "referenda" think the other pronunciation is crass, indicating that the person has not had the very good fortune to study Latin. I use "referendums" … not sure why.

[81] Historical note: More than half the population of Canada live in a province, city or town that has declared itself to be a nuclear weapons free zone, and that hasn't changed anything either.

[82] We also had to endure court challenges to our program in the Supreme Courts of four provinces, Ontario, British Columbia, Alberta and New Brunswick (we won them all—see Chapter 11 of this book, or Chapter 8 of *Cold War Blues* for the full story).

[83] Though one in seven might have Internet access, this access is not evenly distributed around the world. In Canada, one in every two might have Internet access, and in developing countries, perhaps it is only one in every 100, or every 1,000. I realize this is a serious problem for our campaign, but it is not insoluble.

proposition will focus on the *real* issue, the *larger* issue—the creation of a democratic world government, a global governance institution whose role it will be to establish and maintain world peace and the environmental health of the planet *for the rest of human history* ... which we hope will turn out to be millions of years. But what about tactics?

Needless to say, to get the billions of "yes" votes we would require to accomplish our goal, those who *do* have computers and Internet access are going to have to "facilitate" voting by the six out of seven people in the world who *don't* have these technologies, or computer skills.[84] Those with Internet access could invite people to their homes or their offices to vote, or they can get their municipal council to let citizens cast their global referendum votes at the city or town hall, or they can print out paper ballots (from our website, or the Materials section at the end of this book) and help others fill them in and submit them via the Internet, or mail. Newspapers can print the ballot (remember, for the Internet-based referendum, voters have to identify themselves when voting—this is explained in full later) and ask readers to read and think about the issue, vote, and send the ballot to the newspaper or directly to Vote World Government.[85] Magazines can print the ballot with instructions. High schools or universities can conduct mini-referendums using the printed ballots, as could any church, mosque, temple or service organization.[86] At some point we will have to call on legislators, actors, musicians, religious leaders, mayors, sports stars and so on to vote "yes" and to then call upon their fans, friends, co-workers and families to do the same (feel free to do some of this on your own). In fact, we will do anything we can to get the global referendum off the ground.

It is important that these efforts mentioned above be conducted with the utmost integrity. Enthusiastic supporters must take pains to ensure that no stuffing of ballot boxes takes place, and no votes are cast on behalf of unqualified voters (people who are too young, or deceased persons, etc.). It should go without saying that a DWG worthy of universal respect can't be built on a seriously corrupted foundation.

However, this Internet campaign, while it is legitimate and necessary, may prove to be nothing more that a launching pad for the "real deal." If we can get our resolution through the UN General Assembly, then national

---

[84] Having a computer with Internet access doesn't make you better than anyone else, but it does, in this instance, impose on you a responsibility that the majority of people can't accept due to their lack of computers with Internet access.

[85] Or whatever non-profit body is then responsible for the initiative; Vote World Government is a non-profit organization designed only to "kick-start" the global referendum on DWG. It may not endure, or it may not have to endure.

[86] Just before this book went to print, the first mini-referendum was done at City Montessori School in Lucknow, India. Of 7,000+ ballots cast, about 90% were "yes." My thanks to Raj, Dora and CMS for this wonderful result. May 10,000 schools follow your example.

governments would take over the process, and that is how this historic endeavour *should* play out, ideally. (See Appendix #2 for the proposed UN resolution.) However, we can't count on that, so we have to assume that we will have to complete the global referendum on our own, on the Internet and by other means.

Ironically, if we demonstrate that we, the people, *can* probably finish the global referendum on DWG *without* receiving any serious help from national governments, most governments will feel compelled to do a study on what their future prospects would likely be if there *is* a DWG as compared to if there is *no* DWG in place, and there is little doubt that virtually all of them will see that they would have a lot more money for domestic programs *and* far better security for their people if there *is* a DWG, which may cause some of them, and eventually (we hope and expect) most of them, to conduct the global referendum ballot *alongside their next national election*, at a time when voter lists are current and voter fraud is very difficult, if not impossible. There is an old saying that if you start a parade, the politicians will run up to the front and pretend the parade was their idea all along. Let's see if there is any truth in this saying.

> **If leaders won't lead, let the people lead, and the leaders will surely follow.** Benjamin B. Ferencz, *New Legal Foundations for Global Survival: Security Through the Security Council*

> **In our obsession with antagonisms of the moment, we often forget how much unites all the members of humanity. Perhaps we need some outside universal threat to make us recognize this common bond. I occasionally think how quickly our differences worldwide would vanish if we were facing an alien threat from outside this world. And yet, I ask you, is not an alien force already among us? What could be more alien to the universal aspirations of our peoples than war and the threat of war?** Ronald Reagan, to the 42nd General Assembly of the United Nations, September 21, 1987

While this global referendum on DWG has already been started on the Internet (the address is www.voteworldgovernment.org), it's important to note that it will take time. Exactly how much time is impossible to know at this early date, but it may take a decade. If it takes longer, so be it. Once it is rolling, it is reasonable to expect that volunteers will collect ballots for as long as it takes. Of course the speed at which people work on this would go up if there were a flurry of catastrophes around the world (like a local war spinning out of control, floods caused by climate change and perhaps a terrorist attack on some nation's food supply) because destructive human events will underscore the need for reliable and honest global governance.

In tabulating global referendum results over a period of years, we will have to account for voter deaths and the coming-of-age of newly qualified electors. We have tentatively set the minimum age for voting in the global referendum at sixteen. There will likely be other wrinkles and difficulties, but none that can't be dealt with by the World Electoral Commission. The security of the database might turn out to be a problem, for example, but it is not so serious as to discourage us from plunging into the project now, even before we're sure that the online voting system can't be corrupted.[87]

The administrators of the Internet-based global referendum effort will do all they can do to make sure no one votes more than once. However, to provide this assurance clearly means, perhaps unfortunately, that people will not have the luxury of a secret ballot in the first stage of this process. To vote for or against the creation of the DWG, voters will have to say who they are and how they voted ("yes" or "no" to the proposition—see the wording in Chapter 6), and that information will be posted on our website (though *only the first name* of each voter plus his or her country of residence will be publicly visible).

There appears to be no practical way around this, but when you think about it, we stand up for lesser things all the time as a part of being free. People who really want a DWG will have to stand up for this goal publicly, and just overcome any fear they may have of reprisals from those who do not want to give up their right (or their country's right) to make war, or who simply do not care about saving the world for all future generations. However, when the time comes to hold the first global *election* of the DWG, it will *have* to be set up using voter lists and a secret ballot. (This is one of the advantages of having national governments take over the process for the referendum to authorize the creation of the DWG, but if they won't do it, *c'est la vie*; we will just have to do it ourselves, and history will record who helped get it done and who didn't.)

The Internet is a revolutionary tool that will permit us to carry out a global exercise of people-power the likes of which has never happened in the past. The Internet makes it possible for the human race to speak as one, to interconnect, communicate, organize and act on a global basis ... and to publicly demand *and get* what it is that we need most—a lawful end to the

---

[87] Such certainty is hard to come by. It has always been easier to destroy than to create, and never more so than in this age of computers. On November 29, 2007, our entire database disappeared, but we had it backed up, and were able to reconstruct it. It is an unfortunate fact of modern life that some people enjoy using their computers to annoy others or to harm other people, and I expect and trust that a DWG would be involved in the prevention of computer-based mischief and crime.

international state of anarchy and a new institution of democratic global governance that is directly elected and so transparent as to be completely "corruption-free" (see Chapter 5 for more on this last aspect).

At what point can we say we have the required mandate? One third of all people alive today are children under the age of 16, so from the current population of about 6 billion worldwide, 4 billion are adults (16 or older), so if every adult votes, half-plus-one of all adults, 2 billion and one, would have to vote "yes" to say we have the required mandate. However, there is no election or referendum *anyplace* where 100% of all eligible voters actually vote, so let's take a moment to recalibrate. On such a serious matter as this, the half-plus-one formula normally associated with referendums is just not sufficient. To be called a truly compelling global mandate, we should have significantly more than 50% of all votes in the "yes" column, and the total turnout should be as high as possible. (More on these items in Chapter 10.) In addition to the number of "yes" votes, part of the credibility test will be whether there was sufficient time, publicity and facilities to assert that virtually all adults who wanted to vote either did vote or could have voted. Obviously, the spread of the Internet to neighbourhoods in every corner of the world will assist in this mission. Still, I think we should set two billion "yes" votes as our target, our goal, our ideal. (More on this later.)

We can't know ahead of time exactly how history will unfold. If a UN resolution passes and national governments assist us (see Appendix #2), that ideal mandate should be achievable in ten years ... or less. It is even possible that we could collect the entire global mandate in one year if, for instance, a major city went up in nuclear smoke, or if a corporation decided to become "the company that saved the world" by technically facilitating and sponsoring the Internet-based global referendum, or if we figured out how to collect global referendum ballots at warp speed ourselves, perhaps by deploying a multiplier effect, like you'd see in a chain letter or a pyramid scheme. (More on this "multiplier effect" in Chapters 13 and 14.)

> **We are not condemned to repeat the lessons of forty years at the nuclear brink. We can do better than condone a world in which nuclear weapons are enshrined as the ultimate arbiter of conflict. The price already paid is too dear, the risks run too great. The nuclear beast must be chained, its soul expunged, its lair laid waste. The task is daunting but we cannot shrink from it. The opportunity may not come again.** General Lee Butler, Former Commander, Strategic Air Command, speech at the State of the World Forum, San Francisco, October 3, 1996

Chapter 5

Transparency at the DWG

> **To reduce corruption effectively, some features that lead to greater transparency and accountability need to be consciously built into the design.** Subhash Bhatnagar, when working with the World Bank

All types and levels of governments have at one time or another proven to be corruptible, and the *last* thing we need is a corrupt world government. Here's an interesting question: Would we be better off with a corrupt world government or with no world government at all? In my view, we are likely doomed with either of those two options. The third option, the only one that holds any promise for us, is a corruption-free world government.

> **To fight corruption of an international nature, we need an international jurisdiction.** Baltazar Garzon Real, Investigating Judge, Spain, 10th International Anti-Corruption Conference in Czech Republic

It is possible that the global referendum held to authorize the creation of the democratic world government may not get enough "yes" votes to pass unless voters are assured that the new body will be *completely transparent* and therefore free of corruption from day one, *verifiably* so, and that it will remain that way for all time. That's a mighty tall order. Can we achieve and guarantee such a high standard in the new global political structure? And in perpetuity? Can we make ourselves that promise? And could we keep such a promise to ourselves?

Well, we certainly know how to make a government function with total transparency. It isn't even particularly hard, given a modicum of ingenuity and today's wonderful technologies.[88]

You may have heard the political truism that the cover-up is often worse than the original crime. I mention this because each act of corruption in government requires many hidden words, a network of silence and illicit *quid pro quos* among all the conspirators. "Transparency" is the key word in corruption-proofing. It is often used and usually applauded at the UN and

---

[88] The *principle* of total transparency certainly has to be enshrined in the world constitution, but the particulars need not be.

elsewhere, but rarely is it taken too seriously. It is advantageous to be able to express opinions confidentially and privately at times, but at what cost? Most diplomats and politicians are in favour of transparency *for other people*, but not so much for themselves. If we are to have a corruption-free DWG, transparency must be hoisted from its current status (a bit of a joke) to the top of our priority list. And any person who cannot stand that kind of heat should "stay out of the kitchen," as the saying has it.

There is no end in sight to the misuse of power by those in public office…. There is a worldwide corruption crisis. Peter Eigen, (then-) Chair of Transparency International announcing the Corruption Perceptions Index 2001

No company would allow employees to hide vital information from the boss, and in a democratic nation, province or city, "we, the people" are supposed to *be* the boss. And if a DWG is established, I can guarantee that *millions* of "world citizens" will be *passionately* interested in everything that *their* public servants and *their* political representatives are saying or doing, in meetings, on their computers and elsewhere. It is, after all, *their* money, so why not keep tabs? Very *very* close tabs, shall we say.

Secrecy is a form of corruption … lack of transparency is a threat to democracy as lethal as stealing public funds. Oscar Arias, president of Costa Rica and winner of the 1987 Nobel Peace Prize

---

Corruption is an ever-present aspect of the exercise of governmental power and a persistent and often chronic handicap of political life around the world. Richard D. White, Jr. in *Where Corruption Lives*

Like it or not, elected DWG representatives (or global politicians) and senior DWG civil servants should lead recorded lives, meaning they would be "wired" during working hours, and prohibited from discussing DWG business when off-duty (and not wired). In other words, while on duty, they would have to "wear" a voice-activated tape recorder—or, more precisely, the digital equivalent of same.[89]

---

[89] In the February 18, 2007 edition of *Scientific American* is an article entitled "A Digital Life," by Gordon Bell and Jim Gemmell, about new technologies that *can archive everything you hear, speak and see for an entire lifetime*. See also "Total recall," by Clive Thompson, in the *Ottawa*

All these "while-on-duty" recordings (probably thousands of hours of "tape" every day) would then be copied and permanently archived at two separate physical locations. They would be made digitally available to the public from an independent security service charged with transcribing and posting the spoken words on the Internet, as a transcript or in audio form. Transcripts of all recordings should be translated into all *major* languages on an on-demand basis.[90] Computer programs are available that can "machine-translate" written texts into many other languages (these programs are not perfect, but will improve with time). And there are even digital tools on the market (mostly for tourists) that instantaneously translate a person's spoken words to a selected second language, and then "speak" the translation, using a voice synthesizer. All major DWG proceedings could be televised live on a dedicated DWG channel, and archived videos could be made available to anyone over the Internet.

Whoever is careless with the truth in small matters cannot be trusted with important affairs. Albert Einstein

---

Fighting terrorism was dangerous, but fighting corruption was much more dangerous ... The big powers are very strong. Alberto Fujimori, former president of Peru (Ironically, he is now charged with corruption.)

These may seem like wasteful practices until we remember the point of it all. And the task is manageable with new technologies that can store massive amounts of audio, or even transcribe spoken words into print automatically.[91] In these ways, *all* the activities of DWG officials would be *100%* transparent. As well, human nature being what it is, we can know in advance that millions of people and thousands of watchdog organizations will be listening to every minute of recorded audio and poring over all the transcribed words in a search for lies, contradictions, equivocations or even the slightest indication of something scandalous or illegal.

There is no government at any level (that I am aware of) that is clean enough or sufficiently immune from corruption to serve as a model for the

---

Citizen, March 1, 2007, about Gordon Bell, who has totally archived the last seven years of his life. Bell works for Microsoft, and his software is called "MyLifeBits."

[90] The UN has six "official" languages (this applies to all UN organs *except* the International Court of Justice)—English, French, Spanish, Russian, Arabic and Chinese. I expect the DWG would want to aim for translation into *all* languages.

[91] Though not perfectly—all machine-based transcriptions or translations should ideally be proofed by bilingual or multilingual human beings.

DWG. The governmental traditions of the past and present seem to dictate that everything is (or may be) kept secret *unless* there is a very good reason to make it public. There must be a new tradition at the DWG, such that *everything is public unless there is a compelling reason as to why it should be kept private*, and even in such instances, the reason for privacy must be made public, and there must be an affordable appeal procedure whereby a decision to conceal information can perhaps be overturned. The people of planet Earth deserve this level of transparency, and therefore we must insist on it. Anything said or done in the public interest must be public. Anything not public is likely not in the public's interest.

> **Corruption can destroy the strongest democracy if it is not dealt with, so fight it.** Former U.S. secretary of state Colin Powell

We cannot afford "politics as usual" at the world level, and this is the price our DWG representatives will have to pay. It is a small price, and the positive value of this system will very easily eclipse all aspects that might be considered "costs" (financial or otherwise).

We simply must manage our global affairs effectively, and we must manage them in a way that deserves to be called "completely open." The penalty for not doing that may well be that we lose the chance to manage our world at all. We are confident that people will readily adapt to and embrace this kind of complete openness at the DWG. In fact, I fully expect that some people will like it so much they will ask lower-level governments to do likewise.

> **Government is more than the sum of all the interests; it is the paramount interest, the public interest. It must be the efficient, effective agent of a responsible citizenry, not the shelter of the incompetent and the corrupt.** Adlai Stevenson, 1948

In financial matters, the same level of transparency is needed. Every dollar received or spent by the DWG must be posted on the Internet for any amateur sleuth or any forensic accountant to analyze or question. The accounts must show how much money was spent or received, the persons involved in every transaction, and the reasons for the transfer of funds. Every dollar coming in to or going out of the DWG will be "out there," on the Internet. This way it would be virtually impossible for the DWG to get into any financial scandal, and that is what we need at the global level, the cleanest government there could ever be—100% clean. And if science can ever perfect lie-detection, our ability to corruption-proof the DWG would be further enhanced.[92] It would also be desirable and necessary for the DWG to appoint a financial watchdog of its own, like an Auditor General in Canada, whose job it would be to scrutinize DWG financial transactions and to review and report on the success or failure of the DWG's activities.

I repeat; if a person doesn't want this level of transparency applied to his or her professional life, he or she should surely decide *not* to work for the DWG. No one is being *forced* to work under such conditions, but these conditions are necessary at the DWG, for the sake of all.

Corruption hurts the poor disproportionately by diverting funds intended for development, undermining a government's ability to provide basic services, feeding inequality and injustice, and discouraging foreign investment and aid. Kofi Annan, UN Secretary-General, in his statement on the adoption by the General Assembly of the *United Nations Convention against Corruption*

While many people might hesitate to support the creation of a DWG if the new body *did not* have all these seemingly extravagant assurances, now that it seems we are able to set up and maintain all necessary transparency technologies and procedures, there should be little doubt that most people will accept and even celebrate the establishment of the DWG. According to an 18-nation poll (see Appendix #1), most people already do support this goal, but as awareness grows about the possibility of success in the effort to actually establish a DWG, the debate will undoubtedly sharpen, and tougher questions will emerge.

Our insistence on these novel safeguards should assure that the global referendum on DWG gets the highest possible number and percentage of "yes" votes, since we will be guaranteeing ourselves *totally open governance*. We need to remember that scare tactics and a very well-financed campaign of disinformation effectively prevented the public from accepting the science behind global warming for decades, and the same kinds of dirty, dishonest tricks will likely be used to discredit the movement for democratic world government. As suggested earlier, if we do not have all these safeguards or guarantees of integrity at the new DWG, the referendum to authorize its

---

[92] Recent technological breakthroughs seem to indicate that it will not be long before *infallible* lie detection is perfected. Having written a two-book novel on this (*The LieDeck Revolution*), I think the advantages of infallible lie detection will greatly outweigh its disadvantages. Note: In January of 2006, the U.S. Department of Defense called for proposals to develop such a LieDeck-type device, which they call a "Remote Personnel Assessment" device, or RPA. See the work of Dr. Jennifer Vendemia in particular, and fMRI-based experiments in general.

creation might actually fail. Perhaps worst of all, without these safeguards, the DWG *itself* may fail at some point in the future.

Those who corrupt the public mind are just as evil as those who steal from the public purse. Adlai Stevenson, 1952

It is long past time that we used technology to help achieve the goal of squeaky-clean honesty in government. We can't afford a world government, no matter how democratic it is on paper, if it is vulnerable to the corruption that infects all national, provincial (or state) and local governments upon occasion. The choice that we face is probably between a DWG *with* these spectacular guarantees and no DWG—or perhaps some "Big Brother"-type of world government, as anticipated by Tim Flannery (*The Weather Makers*, page 294—more on this later). For this reason, those who are promoting a global referendum on the creation of the DWG want it to be *crystal clear* that a *key* part of the proposal is this revolutionary aspect of total transparency at the world body.[93] To repeat and emphasize—this is not an option; this is a necessity, not because I say so, but for the reasons mentioned above.

The individual is capable of both great compassion and great indifference. He has it within his [or her] means to nourish the former and outgrow the latter. Norman Cousins, American political journalist

---

Some people who read earlier drafts of this book objected to such close scrutiny. They suggested that this practice would create a "reverse onus," where DWG politicians and senior public servants would be "presumed guilty until proven innocent." We know these measures are intrusive, but they only apply to the *official business* dealings of politicians and civil servants, not to their private lives. To argue against these measures seems to defend the right of politicians to lie and cheat, and that is what we would end up with if we declined to "corruption-proof" the DWG—lying and cheating, exactly the way things so often end up at the lower levels of governance.[94] There is no good reason to insist on the right of a global politician or a

---

[93] Transparency is also policy at Vote World Government, the not-for-profit organization behind this initiative, in order to reassure all those who may wonder who we are or why we do what we do.

[94] It is hard to face the fact that dishonesty is quite a natural inclination of our species, even if scientific research and any significant level of observation or perception can confirm this unhappy assessment.

global bureaucrat to be above full professional scrutiny or free to hide facts from the electors who will be, after all, "the boss" of the DWG.

> **Public- and private-sector corruption ... are among the greatest threats to democratic governance.... Public access to State information promotes transparency, [and] is an essential element for combating corruption and an indispensable condition for ... the enjoyment of human rights.** *Declaration of Santa Cruz de la Sierra*, XIII Iberoamerican Summit of Chiefs of State and Government

When you enter many government or corporate buildings, you must sign in, and whether you know it or not, your photograph is taken by security cameras, without your consent. Are they treating you like a felon, or assuming that you are a terrorist until you can prove otherwise? No. Are the post-9/11 security procedures at all airports somehow violating your civil rights or impugning your integrity? I think not, but even if they were, a court challenge would inevitably lead to the judge muttering these words: "Where's the damage?" When you use an ATM, your photograph is taken. Is this yet one more insult to your honour? No. These are simply prudent and necessary security measures, and they serve your *personal* interest as well as the public interest. Similarly, it is in the personal interest of the politician and the civil servant, as well as in the public interest, to have these DWG security measures put in place, for the protection of all voters *and* for the protection of the DWG as an institution *and* ultimately for the protection of the world.

> **No man who is corrupt, no man who condones corruption in others, can possibly do his duty by the community.** Theodore Roosevelt, 1900

Most human beings are basically honest, decent and law-abiding, and that means that we, the "basically-honest-and-decent people," have good reason to be upset. It is outrageous that liars and cheaters so often seem to run the show in modern politics, even in *democratic* politics.[95] This should go without saying, but I will say it anyway: To genuinely "represent" us honest people, a politician must actually *be* honest. We, the honest people of the

---

[95] As reported in the *Ottawa Citizen* of September 23, 2006: "Hungarian Prime Minister Ferenc Gyurcsany stunned the world this week with his comments that his government had lied 'morning, evening and night' in order to win re-election this year. That a politician would lie was no huge surprise—we assume they do it all the time. It was the blunt confession that caught us off guard.... [and] in Hungary, it led to violent demonstrations in the streets."

world, have to stop being a silent majority and become an *insistent* majority. With a system in place to assure complete transparency, we, the people, could even *trust* politicians, something that many of us haven't been willing or able to do for quite a long time.

> **Unthinking respect for authority is the greatest enemy of truth.** Albert Einstein

That having been said, however, we must be on guard against a fortress mentality among our global representatives. Fortunately, there are effective forms of corruption deterrence with few undesirable side effects, like staff rotation, whistle-blowing legislation, very strict limitations on employment following a term in office (no lobbying, no directorships and no consultant fees), and a generous pension, subject to forfeiture for wrongdoing. And of course I must add that all of the transparency and corruption-deterrence measures above should also apply to all the participants in any DWG police force that may be required to carry out a peacekeeping or disaster-response task authorized by the DWG, or to take actions needed to enforce any of the judgements of its judicial arm.

> **It is time to use international co-operation to enforce a policy of zero tolerance of political corruption and to put an end to practices whereby politicians put themselves above the law—stealing from ordinary citizens and hiding behind parliamentary immunity.** Akere Muna, President, Transparency International, Cameroon chapter

Democracy means "government of the people, by the people and for the people,"[96] and you cannot be *for* the people and lie to them. "No lying ever" has to be the rule at the DWG. For a DWG parliamentarian or civil servant to lie to the entire human race must be considered just as serious an offence as a teacher abusing a child, or a policeman dealing illegal drugs.

> **Unlimited power is apt to corrupt the minds of those who possess it; and this I know, my lords, that where law ends, tyranny begins.** William Pitt, Prime Minister of Great Britain, 1770

---

[96] There are many books and essays on what democracy is, but I think it's fair to say that all democrats agree on this basic idea, and I think it is also important to summarize the concept of democracy by using this well-known phrase.

Research indicates that ordinary people tell many lies every single day. One study[97] suggests that the average American tells 200 lies *per day*. Most of these are small lies (often called "little white lies") but still, a lie is a lie, and this number is a shocker. Free people can conduct their *personal* lives however they may wish, within the law. However, at the DWG, we must set things up so that our political representatives and our top bureaucrats *will be caught* by the corruption-proofing system if they lie to us, or to each other, about DWG activities, or about realities at the DWG. And getting caught should be the end of their credibility *and* the end of their careers. World politicians and bureaucrats must maintain the highest levels of integrity, and any serious breach of the people's trust should result in the loss of a career, a pension, and, if the offence warrants it, the loss of one's personal freedom (meaning you go to jail). At the DWG, you simply can't mislead the folks you are paid to serve.

Since corrupt people unite amongst themselves to create a force, honest people must do the same. It is as simple as that. Leo Tolstoy, *War and Peace*

Any intelligent fool can make things bigger, more complex, and more violent. It takes a touch of genius -- and a lot of courage -- to move in the opposite direction. Albert Einstein

---

A zero-tolerance rule for lying may seem extreme or "over the top" at first blush, but consider the consequences of lying and deceptive practices in politics. We, the people of planet Earth, cannot afford to have liars in high political offices if the survival of humanity is at stake, and—as I trust you know by now—that is *minimally* what is at stake. It can't get any simpler than that, so we will do what must be done to assure ourselves that the problem of having dishonest people in politics *does not even come up* at the global level. Lies can no longer be rewarded with power, money or anything else, particularly as we embark on what may well be the "last-chance new beginning"[98] for the human race.

---

[97] By Gerald Jellison, professor of psychology at the University of Southern California, USA. See "200 lies a day keeps chaos away, study finds," by Linda Jackson, *The Daily Telegraph*, London, UK (reprinted in the *Ottawa Citizen*, April 7, 1997).

[98] Or "great turning," as David Korten calls it in his book, *The Great Turning: From Empire to Earth Community*.

> **Every man** [and woman] **possesses the right of self-government.**
> Thomas Jefferson (1743 – 1826; the last words he ever wrote)

After a few decades of corruption-free and totally transparent global governance, I think anyone who says we should discontinue the corruption-proofing aspect or go back to the old system of 194 "completely sovereign" nation states is likely to be laughed at and ostracized, deservedly.

> **We can easily forgive a child who is afraid of the dark. The real tragedy of life is when men** [or women] **are afraid of the light.** Plato

The "rest-of-human-history," if there is to be such a thing, can and must be a time of *unprecedented* integrity ... at least in global politics. If the standard of integrity required at the DWG is not the highest possible, the DWG may fail, and if this were to happen, it follows, almost as a statistical certainty, that humanity will commit omnicide, accidentally or intentionally ... *either* of which qualifies as the most idiotic idea that ever was, or ever will be.

> **Controlled, universal disarmament is the imperative of our time. The demand for it by the hundreds of millions whose chief concern is the long future of themselves and their children will, I hope, become so universal and so insistent that no man, no government anywhere, can withstand it.** Dwight D. Eisenhower, address to the Indian parliament, New Delhi, December 10, 1959

> **Institutions such as a world parliament and a world government would go a long way in eliminating the exclusivism based on race, region, religion and language.** Indian Justice P.B. Sawant, President of the WAPC (World Association of Press Councils), 2004

> **A Parliamentary Assembly would make the UN more transparent, efficient and more democratic.** Boutros Boutros-Ghali

Chapter 6

The ballot proposition

To proceed, we at Vote World Government needed to summarize our goal so as to produce a short, clear question for the referendum ballot. This was not very difficult. There will always be those who disagree, but for now, this wording of the ballot seems the obvious choice:

Do you support the creation of a directly-elected, representative and democratic world government?

As in any referendum, the voters would answer "yes" or "no."

One question that remains is whether the aspect of transparency should be included in the ballot wording. This is easily accomplished by adding the word "transparent" to the list of qualifiers. The ballot question would then read: "Do you support the creation of a directly-elected, representative, transparent and democratic world government?" The consensus *for now* at Vote World Government is that like other important details, such as the key principle of subsidiarity, it isn't necessary to include the word "transparent" in the ballot proposition.

At some point—the sooner the better—there is going to have to be a framing conference to hammer out a constitution for the Earth, where all of these additional aspects would be spelled out in sufficient detail. (The practical implications and mechanics of the three adjectives that are now in the ballot proposition—"directly-elected, representative and democratic"— must also be fleshed out in this founding document.)

There will hopefully come a time when the global referendum voting process is taken over administratively by national governments, as I have suggested in our draft UN resolution (Appendix #2).[99] But that may lead to confusion. Some of those who had voted earlier online might want their online ballot rescinded so they can vote in their national segment of the global referendum, while others may assume their original vote would be counted. This confusion is readily resolved by making it clear that national referendums would supersede the Vote World Government initiative. Thus, governments must advertise the fact that "online" or other votes from the

---

[99] Please note that while we definitely want the governments of nations to assist in the execution of the global referendum, we do not want them to play the pre-eminent role for the rest of the process of establishing the DWG. If they manage to dominate that process, we will end up with the same problems that prevented the United Nations from representing the real interests of the people of Earth.

residents of a country that conducts a *formal* national referendum as its part of the global referendum will automatically be cancelled.

At such a time, there may be a need for reconsideration of the ballot wording, particularly if the draft world constitution has been developed. However, if we get to a place where the UN resolution has been proposed and passed, we don't have to worry unduly about this problem. At that point in time, all of our Internet activities can be seen as merely the means by which humanity compelled its national governments to do what we needed them to do in the first place; i.e., help us get the DWG authorized and established so our national governments can get out of the business of running the world as a whole and get back to what they do best, making *national* laws and applying *national* policies.

(Asking our national governments to run the world is as bad an idea as asking a bunch of mayors to meet occasionally as a way to run a country. Not only will it not work, it wouldn't be democratic, because mayors are not elected to run a nation, only to run a city or a town. Not only are the job descriptions different, but the constant squabbles between the various levels of government make it clear that if these mayors were to wear both hats, they would constantly be faced with conflict of interest situations. This dilemma surely explains some of the difficulties that the UN encounters.)

From now on it is only through a conscious choice and through a deliberate policy that humanity can survive. Pope John Paul II, address in Hiroshima, 1981

There is another issue that needs to be discussed here, and it is this. Some people in the global democracy "movement" (such as it is) think that the referendum ballot should be aimed at achieving not a democratic world *government*, but just a democratic world *parliament*. Right or wrong, in casual conversations, these two words are used interchangeably.

I made the point earlier that "a *government* is not democratic unless it includes an accountable *parliament*, and a *parliament* is of little value unless it can actually *govern*." While strictly speaking, a parliament is not the same as a government, nor is a government a parliament, I do stand by that pervious analysis. I support a world *parliament* in the same way, to the same degree and for the same reasons that I favour a Canadian parliament. And I support a world *government* in the same way, to the same degree and for the same reasons that I favour a Canadian government. (I recognize that once established, a world parliament will likely function much like a national parliament, whereas a world government, once it is set up, will perhaps function more like a city council, whose members are not normally elected to represent a particular political party platform, or a particular corporate or religious agenda.)

The distinction between a parliament and a government is very often overplayed as a bone of contention. I strongly suggest that it can be safely ignored at present while more important issues are settled. I can be *for* a Canadian parliament and *for* a Canadian government, and no one would say a word, but I'm often pressured by some folks in the global democracy movement to make a choice—if I am in favour of one, I should not emphasize or promote the other. Below are some of the arguments I have received for focusing only on a world parliament, and my responses.

1) "World government" sounds too ambitious right now.

That may well be so, but we have made a strategic decision to promote *what we think it will take to fix what is wrong* rather than what people or national governments are most likely to accept. I would rather take that position and fail than find out later that a "parliamentary assembly" created at the United Nations is powerless to change what needs to be changed if the planet is to be saved from human abuse.

There is a campaign for a "United Nations Parliamentary Assembly" (UNPA), organized by the Committee for a Democratic United Nations (KDUN) in Germany.[100] The Board of Vote World Government has now endorsed the UNPA as a "small step in the right direction." However, it is very doubtful that such an advisory or consultative body (which is what the "UNPA" is designed to be) will have any significant influence inside the UN or in the real world. What we now need, and therefore what we should demand and try to achieve, is a bona fide DWG, immediately.[101]

It cannot be said too many times: We are in a true planetary emergency, and we need to embrace a realistic, comprehensive rescue plan now, not in a few years. I might have made a strong argument for the UNPA proposal a decade ago, but not now. In my view, it's too late for half-measures. Way too late.

---

[100] See http://www.uno-komitee.de

[101] In a seminal article, "Towards a Global Parliament" (*The Nation* magazine of September 23, 2003), Richard Falk and Andrew Strauss propose what they call a "Global Parliamentary Assembly" (or GPA), which is essentially the same as the UNPA proposal. One strength of this GPA scheme, they say, is that it is "neither a pipe dream nor a grandiose scheme for world government." Recent alarm over climate change supports the conclusion that we do not have time for the "slow boat to China." Still, the article is interesting, and it can be read at: www.thirdworldtraveler.com/World_Federalism/Toward_Global_Parliament.html. The debate over incremental approaches or shooting for the real deal will likely go on until we either succeed or realize that we are too late for either approach. Let us hope we act in time, as Stephen Hawking suggests in the Preface.

2) The term "world government," or even "*democratic* world government," raises the fear of global totalitarianism.

I have been working for many years (periodically) on another book, tentatively entitled *The Human 3 Evolution*. It deals with fear—where fear comes from, what it is, why we feel it, how it can work for us in some circumstances but other times mess us up, and what can be done when it gets in the way or makes us act *against* our own self-interest, as individuals and as a species. But ... that book is for another day.

> **General fear and anxiety create hatred and aggressiveness. The adaptation to warlike aims and activities has corrupted the mentality of man; as a result, intelligent, objective and humane thinking has hardly any effect and is even suspected and persecuted as unpatriotic.**
> Albert Einstein

We need to be cognizant of fear, and how it can stop progress, and cause wars. We need to remember that some fears are rational and others are irrational.[102] We can't *order* people to stop feeling their irrational fears, but we can create conditions that may convert what had seemed to be a reasonable fear into a less reasonable fear, or render the unreasonable fear un-triggered. For example, Chapter 5 deals with our need to "corruption-proof" the DWG. Some of the proofreaders of this book feared the idea of corruption-proofing, although curiously, they agreed with the goal of total transparency and had no objections to the methodology. It seemed that the actual words mattered, so much so that I changed the chapter's title. (It had been "Corruption-proofing the DWG," which was fine, but it produced a few negative reactions, so I changed it to "Transparency at the DWG," and now the reactions are positive. Go figure.)

Democracy, as practiced today at all levels, is *not nearly clean enough for any global application*. There appears to be no way to build *overwhelming* support for the democratic world government plan *unless* we have the guarantee of total transparency, which is an apparatus that guarantees that no dictator, or authoritarian philosophy, can ever take control of the institution. People's fears simply have to be dealt with. Restricting the executive powers at the DWG is one way of doing that, and the establishment of a foolproof, full-spectrum brand of governmental transparency is another way. I would think

---

[102] There are many hundreds of so-called phobias (a phobia is defined as an "irrational or persistent fear or dread") listed in the medical texts, including a fear of sex, failure, success, high places, closed-in spaces, open spaces, certain colours or of peanut butter sticking to the roof of one's mouth ... and perhaps a baseless fear of democratic world government?

that both are needed. And our irrational fears must be pushed aside, gently or otherwise, as a basis for decision-making.

> **Of course people don't want war.... But after all, it's the leaders of the country who determine the policy, and it's always a simple matter to drag the people along whether it's a democracy, a fascist dictatorship, or a parliament, or a communist dictatorship. Voice or no voice, the people can always be brought to the bidding of the leaders. That is easy. All you have to do is tell them they are being attacked, and denounce the pacifists for lack of patriotism, and exposing the country to danger. It works the same in any country.** Hermann Goering, a Nazi military leader, at the Nuremberg Trials (after World War II)

3) "World government" emphasizes the executive aspect of political power, which makes it possible for power to become concentrated in a few hands, and will cause national politicians to reject the idea.

For some people, the term "world government" *might* imply an emphasis on executive powers (as those exercised by the president of a republic), but "*democratic* world government" does *not* have that implication, for the good reason that democracy (as stated elsewhere) means governance by and for the people. The directly-elected parliament would have the *final authority over all government policies, agencies or departments*. While it may be that a Secretary General and an executive are desirable things to have in a DWG, they would be under the ultimate control of the global parliament.

Nations will likely always exist, since they have many positive qualities. But national governments *are* the problem by virtue of their claim to be the "top-of-the-food-chain" in power. If we are to prevent omnicide forever, *nations can no longer be permitted the freedom to use force to get what they want*. That is one "freedom" the DWG must take away from them (just as the creation of "the nation" took the freedom to go to war away from provinces, cities and individuals). If we are to abolish war, we have to negotiate or arbitrate final solutions to *all* international disputes, and nothing short of a DWG will ensure that that takes place ... and succeeds. In time, national politicians who oppose the creation of the DWG may do so at their political peril. Our job is to design a DWG where power can't *ever* get concentrated in too few hands. I think we can do that job, and do it well ... provided civil society remains vigilant.

Let me return very briefly to the softer approach of a United Nations Parliamentary Assembly. The "UNPA" would be a *parliament-like* gathering of persons drawn from participating national parliaments and modelled on the European Union (which began as a mere advisory board). The UNPA promoters see national governments acting in a manner similar to electoral colleges in the American system, choosing one or more of their own to be the representatives to the UNPA. The "trick" is to switch, later, to a system of *direct* elections (as happened with the EU). However, I must agree with the quote below:

> **There is no first step to world government; world government is the first step.** Emery Reves, *The Anatomy of Peace*, 1945

If a national government is initially opposed to the *direct* election of the representatives to a democratic world government or parliament,[103] that national government is likely to oppose the idea of a UNPA, if only because it advertises itself as a slippery slope kind of a deal—no direct elections at present, but yes, it will have direct elections later on. Even assuming that this sleight of mind works, and that all national governments do permit the emergence of the UNPA, when the day comes to make the "switch" to direct elections, the five permanent members of the Security Council would then have the power—and, I'm sure, the immoveable inclination—to veto that change as many times as it takes for the message to sink in.[104]

> **A parliament at the U.N. would symbolize the notion of humanity as a community of world citizens.** Günter Grass, German writer and social democrat, Nobel Prize Laureate in literature (1999)

If the UNPA came into existence, what do the KDUN organizers say it would do? The UNPA would have a right to "receive information" at the UN, and a right to "make recommendations." This is apparently referred to as a "camel's-nose-inside-the-tent" approach, the theory being that although the start point amounts to very little, over time, the UNPA would acquire greater and greater power. A full list of its proposed powers or rights can be found on the KDUN site, and their rationale for accepting such a modest

---

[103] I expect most national governments will oppose this concept at first, if not for their own reasons, then because the USA or some other powerful national player will pressure them into opposing it.

[104] The initial vote in the UN General Assembly to establish a powerless UNPA requires no changes in the *Charter* of the UN, and therefore does not require Security Council approval. However, when the day comes that the UNPA wants *legislative* power, Security Council approval will be required, and will likely be denied, if not in general, then by means of a veto from one or more of the five permanent Security Council members (likely all five).

start-point is that these limited rights or powers can then be used to apply pressure for further reforms later.

While Vote World Government supports this effort,[105] we have a few concerns about it. First, a "foot-in-the-door" does not always lead to a sale, so we could end up spending a lot of effort trying and failing to acquire something that wasn't what we really needed anyway. Second, I remember this initiative being promoted in the 1970s. Obviously, it has not taken root to date. Assuming a UNPA does come into existence, it may take many decades to grow from a consultative body into something substantial, and we just can't let that amount of time slide by before we make progress on key global agenda items. And third, any political body that does not involve the direct election of its representatives *cannot* be called democratic. I find it extremely difficult to warm up to any world parliament proposal that is non-democratic,[106] even if that characteristic is supposed to be a temporary, hold-your-nose-type expediency.

> **Genuine federalists and world government advocates cannot support the deluded windbags who advocate "reform" or "strengthening" of the UN…. [The UN] needs to be replaced. No amount of reform or "strengthening" of a debating society will convert it into a government.** Harold S. Bidmead, "The Mirage of UN Reform"

The global referendum, on the other hand, is a straightforward power play. It seeks to achieve what it is that we actually need, and it does not depend on the approval of national governments to get off the ground (indeed, it has already begun). If national governments decide how global governance operates, we'll get the UN as it is now, and the failure of the UN to do the job described in its own *Charter* is a fundamental reason why the call for global democracy has arisen. If "the people" have the decision-making power in their hands, we can do a lot better in terms of where we end up *and* in terms of how long it takes us to get there. Given recent revelations about soaring species extinction rates (Google "Red List") plus the possibility that the mid-east wars in Iraq and Afghanistan may lead to a catastrophic WWIII, I think we would be very well advised to demand what

---

[105] I confess part of my motivation for supporting it is practical. I would rather have an UNPA in place at the UN than the UN as it is now. On the tactical side, if the organizers fail to achieve a UNPA (as I expect), they could come to agree that the better approach would be to arrange for the creation of what we actually need, a full-fledged DWG, based on the consent of and an "instruction" from the whole human race, as gathered through a global referendum.

[106] I think the framers of the *Magna Carta* would cringe if they were alive today to witness our timidity.

it is that we actually need, a bona fide DWG, and to recall the words of Carl van Doren, who famously wrote:

> It is obvious that no difficulty in the way of world government can match the danger of a world without it.

In other words, since nations will not do what it takes to repair what we humans have made wrong with the Earth and provide for our indefinite survival, we, the people, have to use the democratic tools available to us, and trust that democracy will prevail. And if we fail, you can be certain that when the world situation starts to come completely unglued, as now seems to be virtually inevitable, powerful national governments and multinational corporations can be relied upon to slap together a very *undemocratic* world government, based on military might ... at which time we will surely weep for the golden opportunity that was lost "back in the early 21st century" to do the job right, to create a *democratic* world government.

In both war and peace, anything less than enough soon proves to be the equivalent of nothing.... The mere existence of a world organization [the UN]**, however inadequate, may cause too many to trust it one day too long, and we may never have another chance.**
Vernon Nash, *The World Must be Governed*

We can be sure that in any DWG, the powers of the executive will be limited, not just because cautious voices will say that would be the prudent way to proceed, but because the governments of nations will never accept the DWG's authority unless it is built in a way that doesn't threaten "their" national sovereignty (except for their "right" or freedom to make war or destroy the environment—those two have to go). As one friend wrote:

> I think we should emphasize the parliamentary and judicial aspect of the new global political order, such as the best part of the experience of the EU [the European Union] suggests. Strictly speaking, there is no European president, but there is an operating legislative body and an EU tribunal [court, or judicial branch].

I simply cannot see how the DWG we propose would be vulnerable to the machinations of a powerful executive if its activities, including those of the world parliament, must take place in a fishbowl, in an environment of total transparently, with a full-spectrum regime of corruption-proofing in play. This "transparency" is a *very* important aspect of our plan. The DWG *must* have this extra safeguard if it is to endure, and it must endure if we are to survive as a species.

Bottom line? The ballot wording presented above should stand. While the proposition or question on the referendum ballot clearly cannot include everything, our wording implies both a democratic world government *and* an accountable world parliament.

The nuclear weapon is obsolete. I want to get rid of them all. General Charles Horner, Commander of U.S. Space Command, July 15, 1994

There can be no real safety against nuclear destruction until the weapons themselves have been destroyed, their possession foresworn, their production prohibited, their ingredients made inaccessible to those who might seek to evade the prohibition.... This view may appear utopian, but to reject it is to accept not only the possibility but the inevitability that someday, somewhere, immense numbers of people will again perish under nuclear mushroom clouds like those that obliterated Hiroshima and Nagasaki 50 years ago.... Wherever, whenever, however many mushroom clouds it may be, we say such an outcome is unacceptable and must be prevented. It can only be prevented if nuclear weapons and, ultimately, war itself are banned from this planet. *Hiroshima Declaration of the Pugwash Council,* July 23, 1995

History is a vast early warning system. Norman Cousins

The atomic bomb survivors ... cannot wait another 50 years. Their highest hope is to see the abolition of nuclear weapons within their own lifetime. It is a steep climb to this goal, but one from which we must never relent. Iccho Itoh, Mayor of Nagasaki, Nagasaki Peace Declaration, 9 August 1995

All war is now civil war. The sluggish general intelligence has still to grasp that fact. World unity under a common law is now ... the only alternative to chaos. H.G. Wells, *Guide to the New World,* 1941

Chapter 7

Taxes

We must all learn to live together as brothers [and sisters] **or we will all perish together as fools.** Martin Luther King Jr.[107]

"How will the democratic world government be financed?" When people ask that question, they generally mean: "Am I going to get stuck with yet another tax bill every year?"

Governments are financed by taxes, so the answer is yes. The DWG will need to raise money to operate, and one way or another those dollars (or yen or roubles, etc.) are going to come out of the pockets of individuals. The DWG will need the power to levy taxes in order to function and do its very important work. And because those who elect members of the global parliament are *individual humans* (not national governments, corporations or other entities), it is entirely appropriate that we should be taxed *directly*. This direct connection is one of the critical safeguards, a reminder to all of us that an MGP's job is to represent the interests of his or her "constituents," and that the global parliament is there to represent the interests of the human race as a whole. So there it is. We will just have to bite that bullet. If you need a new pair of shoes, you know you will have to pay for them. We know we need a democratic world government, and we are going to have to pay for it.

However, there is also some good news that will come as a pleasant surprise. Once you are paying world taxes and the DWG is doing its job, your overall tax bill should *decrease* rather than increase. It doesn't take any advanced mathematics to figure this out—just a bit of basic arithmetic and a dollop of common sense.

Collective security[108] through a DWG will cost only a *fraction* of what it now costs for each sovereign nation to try independently to achieve actual

---

[107] The full quotation reads: "Through our scientific and technological genius, we have made of this world a neighbourhood, and yet we have not had the ethical commitment to make of it a brotherhood. But somehow, and in some way, we have got to do this. We must all learn to live together as brothers or we will all perish together as fools. We are tied together in the single garment of destiny, caught in an inescapable network of mutuality. And whatever affects one directly, affects all indirectly."

[108] The term "collective security" is a good and useful conception. It means that in the same fine tradition of the good municipal police force, in any dispute, the DWG and its agents are not on the "side" of any person or country or group, but on the side of the law (in this case "world law"), and of peace. They will defend all people and the environment against harm-

security against all potential attacks from all other nations.[109] A grab-what-you-can free-for-all is how life really was when every *individual* was, in effect, sovereign. In nature, before tools and civilization, the rule was the so-called law of the jungle, meaning "every man (or woman or family or tribe) for himself (or herself or itself), and the devil (or a predator, more likely) take the hindmost." Our distant ancestors were forever injuring or killing each other over food, mates, beliefs and territories. And throughout history, it was through the *restriction* of individual sovereignty that security was achieved. In spite of the loss of *some* freedoms (the freedom to murder all those who annoy you, for example), our real safety and overall freedoms were *expanded and assured* under the collective security arrangements that were established *within* our cities and nations. No one today would seriously recommend that we turn back the clock and revert to "every man for himself" within all our nations.[110] And the same formula will work among nations once it is made clear that the human race *simply will not tolerate war any more.*

> **Every gun that is made, every warship launched, every rocket fired, signifies in the final sense a theft from those who hunger and are not fed, those who are cold and are not clothed.** Dwight D. Eisenhower

So, although the DWG's taxes will be added to your current tax load, that increase should be *more than offset* by reductions that can then be made in your nation's defence budget. It would not surprise me if, after the DWG has been in operation for a few years, the overall tax load on the average person will be reduced by five percent or more as a direct result of the collective security provided to all of us by the DWG. War would be *against world law*, banned and abolished, and a start would be made in reducing the *ability* of nations to make war, which in every way is far more valuable than *any* amount of saved money. The money now used up by nations to pay for its soldiers and military tools should amount to a huge

doers, and they will enforce *world* law as set out by the DWG ... whenever "enforcement" is clearly required.

[109] For the mathematically inclined, the numbers obviously do not work, if only because most soldiers and machines intended for *defence* can easily be used for *offensive* applications. Indeed, if every nation spent every coin in its treasury on military defence, the world would be less secure, not more—plus there would be no food, no TV, no oil, no golf balls, no beer, no movies, no hospitals, no mail delivery, no Internet, etc., etc., etc.

[110] Well, only the strongest would want to see a system where the strongest wins every time, and considering the humiliations of the USA in Vietnam and the USSR in Afghanistan, it is obvious that "survival of the strongest" doesn't always work when it comes to nations ... unless they are ready to use nukes and/or other WMD ... in which case we *all* lose.

peace dividend for national governments and populations, which could be used to benefit the national population either as a tax reduction, service improvements or as some combination of the two. Collectively, we should be able to leave that "better world for our children" that all people surely strive for, but which we are unable to accomplish as mere individuals.

> **Unless some effective world supergovernment for the purpose of preventing war can be set up ... the prospects for peace and human progress are dark.... If ... it is found possible to build a world organization of irresistible force and inviolable authority for the purpose of securing peace, there are no limits to the blessings which all men** [and women] **enjoy and share.** Winston Churchill, 1947

But how should the DWG levy taxes?

The UN is financed through annual contributions from all its "member states," which is to say from the revenues of national governments. So, the UN administration is dependent on the goodwill of national governments, some of which have, at times, withheld all or part of their dues, attempting to trade that payment for votes for or against some particular policy or UN resolution. No country would *ever* stand for such a gambit internally. You cannot run a nation if some citizens say that they will only pay their tax bill if the government promises to create this or that new law, or promises to change or rescind some other law. It just won't work, and even if it did, that wouldn't be democratic by any definition. The UN often endures a shortage of funds because it can't stop national governments from playing politics with their UN-related financial obligations.

> **The first priority of humankind in this era is to establish an effective system of world law that will assure peace with justice among the peoples of the world ... democracy—civilization itself—is at stake.** Walter Cronkite, American broadcast journalist, best known as anchorman for the *CBS Evening News* (1962-81). Often cited in viewer opinion polls and elsewhere as "the most trusted man in America."

There is a lesson for the DWG in this. It is *not* a good idea to finance DWG operations by taxing national governments. And besides, the DWG's electors are not national governments anyway. They are individuals—adult men and women. If people in all parts of the world are conscious of directly "paying the shot" for the DWG, they will be far more likely to take an interest, perhaps even a keen interest, in how "their" money is being spent.

To reduce bureaucracy, all DWG taxes *should* be collected by national governments in the same way as they collect their national taxes, and such monies would be remitted to the DWG (perhaps with interest on accounts over 30 days late). All monies "collected for the DWG" are *never the property of the national government that collected them.* This is simply a convenient, sensible and cost-effective way of doing things, just as (some) national governments collect taxes for their provincial counterparts.

In regions of deep poverty, a reasonable head tax might be established and paid to the DWG out of the proceeds from the sale of export licenses to purchasers of the nation's natural resources. For special projects (or as a general rule), a DWG should be free to accept no-strings-attached financial donations from governments, corporations, NGOs, charities or individuals … as long as such gifts are subject to all of the transparency or corruption-proofing rules and procedures of the DWG.

Although direct taxation of individuals should clearly be enshrined in a world constitution, the DWG will ultimately decide the *administrative* details of its financing. Still, to reduce the readers' concerns in this area, here are a few more thoughts.

The UN estimates there will be 7+ billion people in the "global village" by 2018. That is a *very* big electorate, which would include about 4.6 billion adults. Now, recalling the fact that most of our political issues are national, regional or local in scope, and the fact that the DWG's authority is limited to supranational issues, the DWG *per capita tax rate* should be quite low compared to national, provincial or even municipal tax rates in developed countries.

Most democracies have a "progressive" tax system. The idea is that the very poor pay no taxes at all, the working poor pay quite a small proportion of their net incomes, middle class citizens pay a higher percentage, and the wealthy pay the highest rate of all. (In reality, significant numbers of the wealthy find legal ways to pay little or no tax, a sad situation that naturally offends those who do pay their fair share.) In today's world, where 3 billion people live on less than $3 U.S. a day, and 1 billion of those live on $1 a day, the DWG would have an administrative nightmare and a unaffordably high cost if it had to check billions of tax returns, and chase down all of the cheaters. So let's look at some other possibilities.

Perhaps a kind of modified flat tax would do. What if every adult in the world with an income level greater than the poverty line (as defined by the national government for any area in question) is taxed at the rate of 0.5% of *net* income? That's just one half of one percent, so a person earning $40,000 (net) a year would owe DWG taxes of just $200 (about *one working day's pay*). Even allowing for defaults and excluding non-earners (meaning those who are young, elderly, disabled or unemployed) from the DWG's tax rolls, a tax rate at that modest level should still be enough to finance the DWG.[111]

The World Bank estimates that the annual gross global income (the sum of gross national products, GNPs, of all nations, although GNP is now referred to as gross national *income*, or GNI) is about $45 trillion. Assuming 50% of 4+ billion adults have paying jobs, that is about 2 billion incomes. The average income would be ($45 trillion ÷ 2 billion working adults =) about $22,500 per year. If all these incomes were over the poverty line, the average amount due to the DWG as tax would be ($22,500 x 0.005 =) $112 per employed adult. The total income then for the DWG (assuming that all adults paid their fair share—a doubtful proposition) would be (2 billion x $112 =) $224 billion. Many people will not pay their fair share, so to be very conservative, let's cut that estimate by half, and say that for this method of financing, the annual budget of the DWG will come to approximately $112 billion. That's *one tenth* of what all countries spend annually on armaments (estimated by SIPRI[112] at *more than $1 trillion per year* for the first time ever in 2004), but still ten times larger than the current UN budget of $11 billion.

Since all people should benefit equally from the services of the DWG, the approach *could* be that every adult must contribute one day's worth of his or her gross income each year to the DWG. All those who are unable to pay anything could volunteer one day of their time to do DWG-approved community service. This would be a miniscule price to pay for permanent world peace and security—a fantastic bargain. Perhaps those who can pay in actual money should *also* do a day of community service every year—if only to say thanks to the DWG for the safe and secure life they would then be enjoying.

Even though the governments of nations should not be required to pay annual dues to the DWG, some may wish to do so anyway. It is not unusual for a person or a government to be "thankful" for something received, and if Canada (for example) was able to cut its military budget by $3 billion per year thanks to these new global security arrangements (a windfall, or peace dividend), some Canadians are sure to call on the government to give some of those savings to the DWG. And why not? Perhaps a contribution *valued* at $1 billion could be made in terms of troops and/or military equipment for a peacekeeping mission, for as long as there are such DWG missions. (Assuming that a world judicial system is working, resolving all outstanding issues and disputes according to world law, there should come a day when

---

[111] Depending on the rate of non-payment of DWG taxes, this tax rate (0.5% of net income) may be too high or too low. I'm not sure there is any math that can nail this down before the DWG is in place. I would encourage others with skills in this area to make the attempt in any event.

[112] Stockholm International Peace Research Institute, and that figure means that $162 is spent on weapons *per year* for each man, woman or child alive.

no military interventions are needed—anywhere. That could happen in less than a century, I think. We must assume that every old or new dispute can be resolved through negotiation, and the DWG must spend whatever time, effort and money are needed to find peaceful resolutions that work.)

> **If nations could only depend upon fair and impartial judgments in a world court of law, they would abandon the senseless, savage practice of war.** Belva Lockwood (1830-1917) U.S. attorney and the first woman to run for president of the United States

Contributions in kind could be made by nations that would not greatly impact on their budgets, but which would greatly reduce the costs of the DWG's operations. Lands presently used for national military training and no longer required for such purposes could be leased (I would suggest very cheaply) for the next 100 or so years to the DWG for the training of its peacekeeping forces or its disaster response teams. The DWG is going to be expected to maintain and upgrade all such properties or facilities, so a country involved in such a deal will earn at least some income from facilities that presently may cost it millions per year to operate ... and that country would also gain a rapid emergency response team "on site." Not a bad deal both ways, I would say.

> **I hope that mankind will at length, as they call themselves responsible creatures, have the reason and sense enough to settle their differences without cutting throats.** Benjamin Franklin, a "Founding Father" of the United States; also an author, politician, printer, scientist, philosopher, publisher, inventor, civic activist and diplomat

A day must surely come when every national government will consider its *voluntary* support for the DWG to be an integral part of the ongoing provision of security to its own population,[113] just as a day must come when all national governments and all people will realize that there is no national security possible without world security, and no world security possible

---

[113] Eventually, security must become a "given" in life, as air is now, and security must be a seamless fabric that stretches from the outer limits of the atmosphere to the kitchen cupboard, from the world to the nation to the city or town or farm or the neighbourhood to the family and the individual and on to the global food supply, the water supply and the environment. This is what has to be done if humanity is to survive, and therefore we must assume that it can be done, and focus our full attention on how to get the job done as soon as possible.

without democratic world government. We have to be prepared to pay whatever it costs. As the old adage has it, "There's no free lunch."

The right to live is ours only if we accomplish our duty as a world citizen. Nationalism is no longer the highest concept. The supreme concept is a world community. Mahatma Gandhi (1869 - 1948)

Where do we begin? What steps can governments take, responsibly, recognizing that policy makers must always balance a host of competing priorities and interests? First and foremost is for the declared nuclear states to accept that the Cold War is in fact over, to break free of the attitudes, habits and practices that perpetuate enormous inventories, forces standing alert and targeting plans encompassing thousands of aimpoints. Second, for the undeclared states to embrace the harsh lessons of the Cold War: that nuclear weapons are inherently dangerous, hugely expensive, militarily inefficient and morally indefensible; that implacable hostility and alienation will almost certainly over time lead to a nuclear crisis; that the strength of deterrence is inversely proportional to the stress of confrontation; and that nuclear war is a raging, insatiable beast whose instincts and appetites we pretend to understand but cannot possibly control. General Lee Butler, Former Commander, Strategic Air Command, speech at the State of the World Forum, San Francisco, October 3, 1996

Our defense is not in armaments, nor in sciences, nor in going underground. Our defense is in law and order. Einstein, 1964

Nationalism is an infantile sickness. It is the measles of the human race … As a citizen of Germany [before WWII], **I saw how excessive nationalism can spread like a disease, bringing tragedy to millions …
I** [have no] **special attachment to any state or national entity whatsoever.** Albert Einstein

Peace and justice are two sides of the same coin. Dwight D. Eisenhower

Chapter 8

Implementation

> **Those advocates who work for world peace by urging a system of** [democratic] **world government are called impractical dreamers. Those "impractical dreamers" are entitled to ask, "What is so practical about war?"** Walter Cronkite

Even a strong species-wide mandate resulting from a global referendum will not *automatically* create the reality described in the proposition on the ballot. When and if the global referendum is finished, and assuming the collected ballots indicate a solid majority in favour of the DWG, several real hurdles remain before we can sit back with a hot cup of fresh coffee and watch the inaugural session of the new world parliament on TV.

> **The only way to escape our dilemma is to put world law above the national governments, and to make a parliament to create such world law, we need to constitute this world parliament by way of global elections in which all people will vote.** Albert Camus

Before the first general election of Members of the Global Parliament (MGPs) can take place, the geographic areas of the DWG constituencies will have to be defined, or at least *tentatively* decided upon, as fairly and reasonably as possible. Because we are talking about the architecture of a *democratic* world parliament, the basis for political representation within the DWG must be by population—or "rep by pop," as the saying has it. No other basis affirms the political equality of all people, and because that principle is so important for all true democrats, no other basis is needed.[114] While DWG constituencies will vary in geographic size, all constituencies in any particular country should be of approximately equal size *in terms of how many people are in them.* So, what are the challenges?

---

[114] There are schemes to "weight" the votes of nations at the UN, but we are not talking about reforming the UN. We are building a DWG. Having said all this, other ideas can be considered to ensure that insofar as it is possible, significant cultures or unique geographic areas are either represented or given a voice in the DWG proceedings. These matters will ultimately be dealt with not by an un-elected Electoral Commission, but by the drafters of the world constitution or, better yet, by the DWG itself, a little later.

Let us begin with what has already been decided (or proposed), the idea that there should be about 700 DWG constituencies in the world, each with a maximum of ten million people. It would be foolhardy to try to assign people from two different countries to the same DWG constituency (I trust we can all agree to that), so adjustments have to be made.[115] As well, even the smallest nation should have one MGP (even though the DWG's "membership" is not based on national entities). So, how would "rep by pop" apply at the world parliament/DWG?

Here is the obvious solution. Every MGP will get ten or fewer votes in the DWG—one vote per million people represented. All constituencies will be home to 10 million people or less, and it will be neater by far to have MGPs holding from one to ten votes than it would be to have most MGPs possessing only a fraction of a vote each. If there are seven billion people in the world at the time this plan is implemented, that's 7,000 million people, and that translates into 700 (or so) MGPs, collectively possessing 7,000 (or so) votes.[116]

In addition to the wrinkle where each nation has at least one MGP with one vote even if that nation's population is less than a million, it would be best if multiple MGPs from one nation split up all of the available votes evenly. Thus, a nation of 10 million citizens (rounding up or down to the nearest million) would have just 1 constituency, and the people there would be represented by 1 MGP, who would have 10 votes. A nation of only 9 million people would have 1 constituency, and 1 MGP with 9 votes. A nation of 11 million would have 2 constituencies, and 2 MGPs with 11 votes in total, which comes to 5.5 votes per MGP (or per constituency). And of course a nation of less than 1 million people would still get one MGP, with 1 vote. (There are at this time 38 countries with less than one million people, so the number of MGPs rises from 700 to *about* 738, and the number of DWG votes goes from *about* 7,000 to *about* 7,038. These numbers can be refined and pinned down later, at the time when we have to know *exactly* where we stand within every constituency.)

Based upon *and deriving from* that first assumption (of 700 constituencies globally), and with the application of the reasonable principles mentioned above, it was not too difficult to work out the representation situation for every country in the world. This work is presented as a chart in Appendix #3. You can go there at any time, look up your own country and catch a

---

[115] Those who wish to ignore national boundaries are simply not dealing with the situation realistically, in my opinion. It may take a couple of generations before national hostilities calm down in the hearts and minds of all people, so if and as our descendants reach such a point in the future, they can re-slice the political pie again, however they may want.
[116] The two "(or so)" interjections in this sentence result from the adjustments that will have to be made for the smallest countries with populations of less than one million.

glimpse of your future representation, as it would be under this rescue plan.[117]

Here are the first ten entries from the chart in Appendix #3, so you can see how this would be done

1	2	3	4
Countries (in alphabetical order)	**Population** in millions <u>and</u> **# of DWG votes**	**Number of constituencies** and **MGPs**	**Number of votes per MGP**
1 Afghanistan	29	3	(29 ÷ 3 =) 9.7
2 Albania	4	1	4
3 Algeria	32	4	(32 ÷ 4 =) 8
4 Andorra	0.07	1	1
5 Angola	11	2	(11 ÷ 2 =) 5.5
6 Antigua and Barbuda	0.07	1	1
7 Argentina	39	4	(39 ÷ 4 =) 9.75
8 Armenia	3	1	3
9 Australia	20	2	(20 ÷ 2 =) 10
10 Austria	8	1	8

I am a Canadian, and with a national population of 33 million, Canada would be entitled to 4 MGPs, one from each of 4 constituencies. And those MGPs would have 33 votes (1 vote for each million citizens, remember?) in total, so every Canadian MGP will have (33 ÷ 4 =) 8.25 votes. But how do we draw those four constituencies onto a map of Canada?

The start point, logically, should be by means of computer modelling. Please note that computer modelling is not being suggested as the *only* step in the process, just a way to get things started.

Since Canada is wider (east-west) than it is tall (north-south),[118] a good computer modelling program could then be asked to draw in three vertical (north-south) lines that divide the nation into four geographic areas of equal populations (8.25 million people each, to be exact). In another country of 33 million that is more round in shape, a centre point can be located, and four lines could radiate out from there that would have the same effect—like a pie-chart, where each "slice" is different in geographic size, but equal

---

[117] The number of constituencies and votes, as well as constituency boundaries, may be revised by the DWG at the time of each future election of MGPs, say every 5 or 10 years or as required in the world constitution, to reflect shifts in population since the last DWG general election.

[118] Or at least it seems that way, since the *vast* majority of our population lives within a few hundred miles of the USA, to the south, and the huge far-north territory is hardly populated *at all* compared to the southern regions of Canada.

to all others in population. If the population of some other round-ish nation is 55 million, it would be divided into six constituencies of (55 ÷ 6 =) 9.17 million people each, so the centre point would have six lines running out, making six "wedges." In the case of a particularly large country (say 75 million or more), the computer-modelling program could establish a grid where all eight "squares" (although some will be tiny compared to others, and some may be quite misshapen) contain the same approximate number of people (whatever the number is, it must be less than ten million).

This is not difficult! I emphasize that because inevitably, some people will try to make it sound virtually impossible, for whatever reasons. Hopefully, those people who have the skills, the computer modelling programs and the required population-distribution databases will apply their various skills and technologies to this situation so we can get the DWG show on the road.

Learn from yesterday, live for today, hope for tomorrow. The important thing is to not stop questioning. Albert Einstein

---

With all 700 or so *tentative* political constituencies drawn onto maps, we can make these maps generally available so that those living in any particular constituency will be able to study their boundaries and comment on their appropriateness. But if you were displeased, what body would you complain to? And computer modelling requires access to population databases that some "developing" countries may not have (except as rough estimates). As well, even where databases are available, what we would get is a mechanical result, a result that is technically correct, but which doesn't respond to real life circumstances. Those computer-generated boundaries won't deal with annoying geographic features such as mountain ranges or rivers that may bisect a constituency, nor will they deal with or reflect cultural or religious differences among all of the people who live in a region. What to do?

Let us return momentarily to the example of Canada, and assume that the national government is entirely cooperative in the process by which the people of the world are forming this new political entity, the DWG. (Such a situation would be wonderful, but is not likely to exist until or unless there is clear evidence that the people of Canada want it to happen, and will do it *without* the cooperation of the national government if that is the only way to get it done.) What difference does this imagined governmental cooperation make in terms of defining where the boundaries of these four Canadian DWG constituencies are to be drawn?

Canada has 33 million people, and 308 MPs (Members of Parliament), which means there are also 308 constituencies—these are called "ridings" in countries that follow British traditions. If we divide 33 million by 308, we learn that an *average* riding in Canada has *about* 107,000 people.[119] So rather than accept lines drawn on a map by a computer modelling program, we can focus in on the fact that we need four DWG ridings, and we could have their boundaries conform to the outer edges of a group of existing national riding boundaries. In other words, there would be (308 ÷ 4 =) 77 national ridings in each DWG constituency. The easternmost 77 national ridings would constitute the first Canadian DWG constituency, the next 77 ridings to the west would then constitute the second DWG constituency, the next 77 ridings to the west would constitute the third DWG constituency, and the last 77 national ridings, ending at the west coast, would constitute the fourth Canadian DWG constituency. The three dividing lines wouldn't be exactly straight anymore, but that doesn't matter as long as we end up with four DWG constituencies of roughly equal populations. Still, why would we do all that? Where's the advantage?

If the Canadian government is cooperating with the effort to establish a DWG, it will surely allow the national segment of the global referendum—the one to authorize the creation of the DWG—to take place *in tandem with a Canadian national election* (as well as any future global referendums that may be needed). But with the DWG constituency boundaries adjusted to match groupings of *national* ridings, the government of Canada can also allow the first DWG *general election* to proceed in this way, and a person voting for his or her next member of the national parliament will be able to vote *at the same time* for his or her choice of an MGP. (In an ideal world, every nation would proceed this way, but … well, we don't have an ideal world.)

Bear in mind that official decisions on constituency boundary issues will ultimately be the responsibility of the DWG … *once it is elected*. Still, we should not miss the chance to be as fair as possible prior to that first global election. And besides, there has to be some sort of an electoral commission to decide matters *other* than these constituency boundaries prior to that first DWG election, so that electoral commission could also deal (as best it can) with the issue of boundaries. Let us then try to find a reasonable way of choosing the participants for such an electoral commission, and never lose sight of the fact that the elected world parliament, once it is constituted, will have a formal judicial appeal process within which *all* of the decisions of the electoral commission can be reconsidered and revised at a later date.

Before there is a world parliament, then, we have to establish a World Electoral Commission to prepare for and to manage the first global general election of representatives (MGPs) to the DWG (among other duties), and we must create a world constitution to serve as the foundation, the primary

---

[119] The size of the populations of ridings are not all the same, of course, as populations do move about or grow, and when these variances get too pronounced, parliament re-draws the electoral map to reflect the changed conditions.

world law upon which all else is built. While the constitution is dealt with in Chapter 12, this idea of a World Electoral Commission must be dealt with here and now.

As the referendum votes are rolling in (as a result of online voting or by other means), perhaps when we are one third of the way through, and assuming we are getting a strong "yes" vote from people all over the world, we face the problem of how to select these representatives to the World Electoral Commission. In each country, there will be (we now assume) one constituency for every ten million (or fewer) people, and those constituency boundaries will obviously *not* be the same as the constituency boundaries that are used for national, provincial or local elections, where the numbers of people per constituency would be a lot smaller.

The World Electoral Commission is a precursor to the DWG, so let's assume it should therefore have as many members as the world parliament would have MGPs (Members of the Global Parliament). This produces a theoretical World Electoral Commission of 700 (or so) persons. That un-elected body must approve (by majority vote) the constituency boundary decisions coming from the smaller group of electoral commissioners in a given country. In Canada, for instance, there would be four World Electoral Commission members, one from each DWG constituency. They can decide among themselves where those three near-vertical lines should go, based on the computer modelling decision and their best efforts to adjust the lines according to legitimate objections or complaints (from individual citizens or from other parties in Canada, including religions or language groups, service organizations, cities, provincial governments, the federal government or any other body). If the four commissioners can't agree on a recommendation of boundaries for Canada, then the World Electoral Commission will have no choice but to fall back upon the boundaries that were computer-generated, and leave the final adjudication until after the DWG is in place.

But how would we select the four Canadians who would make up our *national* group of commissioners? Insofar as these commissioners would be selected, and not elected, how do we pick out four in Canada, and how do others do similarly in their nations? Insofar as neither commissioners nor MGPs represent nations, it would be wrong to allow any national Chief Electoral Officer to make the selections alone. However, since any nation's commissioners would be members of the World Electoral Commission and since the World Electoral Commission must deal with issues such as voter eligibility, minimum age, scrutineering (the observation of a voting process to assure fairness and prevent duplicate votes), the Chief Electoral Officer of that nation (or of any provinces or cities within that nation) can certainly advise on these and other related matters. Which brings us back to how we select the electoral commissioners.

Municipal councils are the governments closest to the people, and the DWG is a people-powered initiative. Therefore, my recommendation is that the council of the biggest city in any constituency take the decision as to who will be the World Electoral Commissioner for that DWG constituency. In other words, once the computer model has set the boundaries for the four constituencies that exist inside the nation of Canada, for instance, each of those constituencies would have an obvious largest city, and that city's council can call for nominations, and choose from among all the submitted names. (Retired diplomats, judges or scholars might be good choices.)

The electoral commissioners who are thus selected can then connect with each other by phone, email or Internet conferencing tools, so for most purposes they do not need to travel to a single geographic spot to get on with their work. The four in Canada should not only be in touch with each other, but also with the World Electoral Commission's central office. And if these four can agree on the boundaries for Canada, there is no reason why the World Electoral Commission should not affirm that recommendation. Similarly, the electoral commissioners of other nations will have to agree on a submission to the World Electoral Commission, or face the necessity of accepting the computer-generated model that was done as their start-point.

This World Electoral Commission exists for only two purposes—to get constituency boundaries settled worldwide, and to be sure the first global election of MGPs goes ahead smoothly.[120] The 700 (or so) members of the World Electoral Commission will need an office and dozens of employees to conduct their business (in many languages), and the UN could help if it chooses to, as can the member states of the UN. Even though all decisions of the World Electoral Commission will be revisited by the DWG at such time as the first group of MGPs are elected, it would be good if the UN helps the World Electoral Commission get off to a positive start. A nation's ambassador to the UN could use the facilities of the UN mission (the UN term for "embassy") to help the electoral commissioner(s) from his or her country get to work. If the government of a particular nation is opposed to the emergence of the DWG and will not allow its UN ambassador to assist in the process, other ways will be found to get the electoral work for that nation completed, and history will record who helped and who didn't.

Besides the obvious list of duties mentioned above, the World Electoral Commission may also establish independent panels to study ideas intended to protect the interests of people living in disputed areas, and of nomadic populations (the Inuit, Laplanders), and the interests of unique geographical areas (like Antarctica, the Sahara and the Brazilian rainforest). Additionally, the World Electoral Commission could appoint "voices," people who can

---

[120] Related duties were mentioned earlier, such as establishing the minimum age for voting, nomination eligibility, voting procedures, etc.

speak for the oceans of the world, or endangered species, or threatened ecosystems. But all these aspects do not have to be finalized here and now, and are best left to others as the process of forming a DWG goes forward. There are endless ideas, I'm sure, and all likely have some merit, but for the period of time before the first general election, all such ideas that can't be easily resolved have to yield to the critical timetable that will determine how quickly the DWG can be elected and get into the work of ending war and preparing to resolve our rather long list of pressing supranational problems. It should not take more than a few years to get from the global mandate (for the establishment of the DWG) all the way to the reality of the DWG, even if problems pop up that tend to slow events down.

> **A federation of all humanity, together with a sufficient measure of social justice to ensure health, education, and a rough equality of opportunity, would mean such a release and increase of human energy as to open up a new phase in human history.** H.G. Wells, *The Outline of History*, 1922

The manner in which the first general election is held has to be spelled out in the world constitution. Those who draft the world constitution (see Chapter 12) will have to make decisions about the *principles* involved, and I expect that there will be many lessons learned from the first global voting experience (the global referendum to authorize the creation of the DWG). Later, before the second global voting effort is done (to elect the first full slate of MGPs), a draft constitution should have been openly constructed, so voters can approve or reject it in a referendum that would (hopefully) be conducted *at the same time as the first general election* of MGP's. Legislation by the resulting world parliament can refine the electoral process at any later date, and perhaps even integrate new voting-related corruption-proofing technologies as they become more reliable and ever more affordable.

If the world constitution is not ratified as the result of this vote, it must be remembered that humanity has still decided to create the DWG, so the MGPs that are elected would still have to go to work, but instead of diving into the *real* global issues (banning war and protecting the environment), they will have to figure out why the draft constitution failed, and prepare a second draft constitution for voters to consider at a later date. Although this scenario would result in a very significant delay, it is a price we must be prepared to pay to maintain the principles of democracy.

Let's assume here that the global referendum to establish the DWG is basically completed by 2014 or 2015, and passes handily. We had set 2018 as the target date for the first global election. Let us additionally assume (for now) that a draft world constitution is *not* available for ratification in 2018. (It really should be ready, since writing a constitution is just not as hard as it is commonly thought to be.) So, the vote in 2018 would be held for the sole purpose of electing the 700+ MGPs. Here are three options for getting that voting done.

1. Have every country prepare to accept DWG votes on paper ballots at the same time as (meaning "in tandem with") its 2018 (or its "next-after-2018") national election, using all the polling stations and official voters' lists that will be used in that national election.

2. Have all adults in the world vote, using paper ballots, on a single day (or maybe over a three-day weekend), *not* in tandem with any country's national elections, but using official voters' lists from the most recent or next national election (as available).

3. Create a system of electronic, Internet-based voting, and allow each monitored polling station to stay open for perhaps two months, so no one can say they did not have ample opportunity to study and discuss the issues, or ample opportunity to vote.

Those first two approaches probably won't work. For one thing, some countries don't have fair national elections, and for another thing, a national government that opposes the idea of establishing a DWG (and there may be dozens) could simply refuse to allow the use of its national voters' lists. Either way, these first two approaches can't be the *main* approach, as they are just too easily thwarted. This does *not* mean we should back away from our effort to have a UN resolution passed calling for a nation-by-nation "in tandem" approach to the first global referendum. Some countries may do it this way *even without the blessing of the General Assembly*, and Internet voting can be employed to handle the rest of the world. As for doing a global general election this way, it would be most cost-effective if global general elections and global referendums were to be *administered* by national governments. In today's chaotic world, however, we must go with what is most reliable, and try for what is ideal later.

That analysis leaves us with electronic voting as the *main* approach. In 2008, there are serious questions about the integrity or reliability of Internet voting systems. I've been assured by one expert on emerging technologies that by 2018, we will have technologies with which to assure ourselves and everyone else that the voting process has not been corrupted.[121] While such

---

[121] Ted Stalets, who has set up hundreds of websites on "emerging technologies" (robotics, biotechnology, nanotechnology, virtual reality), geared for the non-technical person, wrote:

a system may not be 100% feasible or affordable today, it will be *both feasible and affordable by the time that we need it*. Also, now that we have announced our anticipated need for such technologies and systems, surely some scientists will look at this precise application, and make certain the technology we will need *is* there when we, the people of Earth, need it.

This process of Internet voting could take some time to finish, since monitors and technical experts might have to move from one constituency to another every so often (or move from one location to another within a constituency). If we want all adults in the world to have voted via the Internet in one year, and each monitoring team requires two months to cover a constituency of up to 10 million, each team would be able to do 6 constituencies in one year, and the need would be for approximately (700 ÷ 6 =) 117 such teams. To adequately cover a constituency of say 9 million people (this translates to 6 million adults, or eligible voters, assuming that the minimum voting age is 16) would require a sizeable team of monitors and technical experts, as well as locally-enlisted scrutineers.

There is no sense denying that the logistics and costs of this effort are daunting, and for that reason alone, every effort will be made to get national governments to not only *permit* the DWG general election to take place in tandem with national elections, but to foot the bill for it as well. If ordinary people and civil society are getting the global referendum done at a pace that says it will be completed in a few years, national governments will sense that this represents a "sea change," or a political "paradigm shift" that will change everything, forever. Some governments will realize that it is in their own interests not only to allow this operation to take place on its territory and among its population, but also to encourage it, in words and in deeds. It is my expectation that with luck, a third of all nations, perhaps as many as half, will conduct the DWG general election alongside a national election. (I must also point out that while this method saves a lot of money and effort, it may *add to the total time* that it takes to complete the general election for the DWG, since the date set for the next national election in any country is not going to be changed just to suit the DWG effort.)

Speaking of money, I remember reading in history class about how the Canadian government sold "war bonds" to finance WWII. Perhaps we at Vote World Government, or the coalition we hope will promote the DWG, could sell bonds of a more positive ilk—"peace bonds." Or maybe the first major infusion of capital to the DWG (which could perhaps be paid to the

---

"Methods used in the science of biometrics are already quite sophisticated, [and] ... we will have the required technologies to identify the uniqueness of individuals and authenticate unique votes well within the next ten years." He added that on the physiological side of biometrics (as opposed to the behavioural side), "there are now reliable scans of fingerprints, faces and eyes [no two irises are identical], and any of these could be used to assure the integrity of DWG votes in global referendums or global general elections."

UN in trust) will come from ordinary people who decide to start paying their DWG taxes before they are required to do that. This kind of altruistic behaviour doesn't sound like many of the people you know at the moment, I'm sure, but if the deep sense of urgency that drove this initiative spreads to the folks who live on "Main Street, Earth," we may discover that millions of people are willing to pull together and make financial sacrifices for the protection of their actual "homeland," Earth.[122] If neither common sense nor fear does the job, maybe self-interest is a proper motive for backing the DWG. I don't particularly like the sound of that notion, but that does not mean it won't be a part of the bigger picture. Self-interest is a *very* powerful and reliable motivator, and assuring the avoidance of one's death, including a "death by omnicide," is perhaps as self-interested as one can get.

The people of the world must understand the forces driving them toward the coming holocaust. It has nothing whatever to do with Communism or capitalism, with individualism or collectivism. It is the inevitable conflict between non-integrated sovereignties [nation states] **in contact.** Emery Reves, *The Anatomy of Peace*, 1945

The political obstacles in our path are formidable. We know that. The toughest nut to crack may well be the badly misguided belief by national governments that if they "surrender" even a tiny bit of the sovereignty that they assume to be theirs,[123] they would thereby be "surrendering" some freedom or security. It is difficult for national governments and for most politicians to realize that in spite of their best efforts to achieve national security, the old system of multiple, separate and "non-integrated" national sovereignties is at the heart of their indisputable failure to ensure national security. It will take a little time for individuals and governments to gain their "civilized-world legs," to understand that from now on, the *only* road to real national security is through a global system of collective security, a security paradigm as new as democratic world government itself, organized by and for all the *people* of Earth. If we believe in government, as surely we do, and if we believe in democracy, as surely we do, then we must also believe in this new idea of a democratic *world* government. And if we have

---

[122] The outpouring of financial assistance to tsunami victims was estimated at an astonishing $13 billion! "South Asians mark tsunami anniversary," UPI, June 26, 2005. If it were to be well understood that creating the DWG is necessary for the survival of oneself and one's children, this number of dollars could well be surpassed.

[123] This is not to suggest that nation states have used that particular bit of *our* sovereignty wisely or well, nor is it to concede that sovereignty "belongs" to the nation state, or to any national government (see Chapters 10 and 11).

made that connection, that conceptual leap, then we must create a DWG, and make it work, starting with security.[124]

> **Social justice cannot be attained by violence. Violence kills what it intends to create.** Pope John Paul II

It is not very difficult to get your mind around this new-to-some idea of collective security. It is a phenomenon everyone is familiar with on the local level. The global security system should parallel the way that the best police force, controlled by a democratically-elected local council, achieves security within a city, but applied three governmental levels up, and with the special safeguard of the corruption-proofing technologies and techniques that were presented and discussed in Chapter 5. Most people already understand why it is that no citizen can be permitted to arm himself or herself to the point where he or she could annihilate an entire neighbourhood, even if we must concede that it is *theoretically* possible that the neighbourhood is planning an attack against that person's house. In this situation, what happened to the individual's "right to bear arms," to this person's right to defend himself or herself? Self-defence is something of a "sacred right," is it not? (Small wonder that courts are forever trying to balance out a host of competing rights and find compromises that work—it's easy to argue and disagree, and people seem to enjoy doing it.)

> **War remains the decisive human failure.** John Kenneth Galbraith, influential Canadian-American economist, a leading proponent of 20th-century American liberalism and progressivism

The "right" of any individual (or household) to "self-defence" is limited because it is clearly "outweighed" by the collective right of all individuals to live in a city or town that is not bristling with a stockpile of weapons that would be appropriate only for a war. We all know that trusting the police to be against the aggressor and on the "side" of the victim is as good as it gets in terms of *actual* physical security, even if some people might feel a lot safer

---

[124] Issues of justice and the shared environment must not be forgotten, but they are just a lower priority than security, and will take some time and great effort to resolve. Security—freedom from violence and war—is likely the easiest item to finalize, even though (like police forces even in the best democracies) there will be a constant need to stay on top of the situation, a need that will likely endure forever. And as Kofi Annan said (in Kenya, November 15, 2006), climate change is an "all-encompassing threat," so it is not a stretch to see that it could well (in Annan's words) "imperil global security."

with machine guns pointing out all their windows and landmines planted in their front yards. Allowing that kind of "sovereignty" on the individual or the household level leads us into anarchy and chaos on the larger level, and is therefore not permitted so that a good measure of *community* security can be achieved (and, by extension, more actual meaning can be injected into the term "national security"[125]).

Even if we are spared destruction by war, our lives will have to change if we want to save life from self-destruction. Aleksandr Solzhenitsyn, Russian novelist, dramatist and historian; awarded the Nobel Prize for Literature in 1970

Just as us individuals prosper best in disarmed neighbourhoods, nations will have a lot more *real* sovereignty, *real* security and *real* prosperity after the establishment of the DWG, compared with what they had before. But there is simply no way around the stark fact that some restrictions on national sovereignty are going to be part of the "package" by which humans finally achieve world sovereignty and world security.

There will be clarion calls for caution, and there will be lots of serious fear-mongering, but by the time those noises die down, we will be left with the same equations, and the same choices. Theoretically, it should become increasingly hard to sell any rationalization for any war based on traditional fears as humanity moves away from the "jungle mentality" and embraces "civilization" to the fullest. And yes, this road will likely be bumpy. Some people will try to hang on to the past, but those who do will surely fail, if only because it will be obvious to almost all people that it makes no more sense to object to the idea of a democratic *world* government than it would to object to a democratic *national* government, or to a democratic province or municipality or trade union or chess club, for that matter.

We need national governments to do important things, just as we need provincial and municipal governments to do many other important things. It is patently absurd to suggest that a sensible adult would even *consider* the possibility of dismantling governments at these levels. Now, because of the new implications of technology (plus a host of other compelling reasons), we absolutely must civilize our whole world—not just at the local, regional and national levels, but at *all* levels. With a democratic world government in place, we will at least have the opportunity to try, and arguably a very good

---

125 Question. How much does national sovereignty or national security *really mean* if there are 190+ foreign countries, plus non-state terrorist groups, that can get their hands on WMD and use same to wipe your country off the map in an afternoon, or a month? Answer. Very little; perhaps no meaning at all.

chance of succeeding. Without a democratic world government, we will not even have a chance of *surviving*, as Albert Einstein bluntly said.[126]

> **It is incontestable that the [U.S.] Constitution established a system of "dual sovereignty." ... Although the States surrendered many of their powers to the new Federal Government, they retained a residuary and inviolable sovereignty ... The Framers explicitly chose a Constitution that confers upon Congress the power to regulate individuals, not States. The great innovation of this design was that our citizens would have two political capacities, one state and one federal, each protected from incursion by the other.** Unknown. Source: U.S. Supreme Court, 1997, Printz v. United States [Interior quotes & citations omitted]

The addition of a democratic world government to the planet's political landscape does not negate national sovereignty—except insofar as nation states will no longer be allowed to make war or destroy the environment. Of course there will be very healthy debates over what is and what is not a "supranational issue," and there will be some overlaps and commonalities to complicate life, but in essence, we should end up with a system of dual sovereignties. You and I will be a citizen of the world, but also a citizen of a nation state ... and a province and a municipality, too.[127] But while most individuals do not become too emotionally attached to cities or provinces, and change those addresses at will, moving to another country is a *very* big deal (and moving to another planet isn't even an option). The two "biggies" are one's allegiance to a nation state and one's love for the planet Earth, and while it is inevitable that at times these two attachments may lead us into conflicting sentiments, that circumstance is not terribly different from the occasional complications that arise from loving your parents and loving your kids too. These are just different kinds of love, both valid, and rarely in conflict, but when they do collide, we just take a deep breath and find a way through or around the problem. Sure, politics is never as warm and fuzzy as good family relations, but in politics, too, if there's a will, there's a way. The DWG is there to represent our will to resolve our disputes without killing

---

[126] For those who forgot, he said: "There is no salvation for civilization, or even the human race, other than the creation of a world government." And for the few who don't know, he was considered a world-class genius, and he was chosen as *Time* magazine's "Person of the Century" (the 20th century).

[127] Remember the principle of subsidiarity, mentioned earlier, which states that all issues should be dealt with by the smallest *appropriate* level of government. This idea of subsidiarity is a "must include" item for the world constitution (see Chapter 12). It should also be noted here that some people (very few, to be sure) already have "dual citizenship" in relation to national identities.

each other, and our will to protect the planet against human abuse. That is what we need, and I expect that is exactly what we are going to achieve in the next decade or three. So, let us now return to the main purpose of this chapter, the implementation of a plan that we think and believe the human race will vote for.

> **This world of ours … must avoid becoming a community of dreadful fear and hate, and be, instead, a proud confederation of mutual trust and respect.** Dwight D. Eisenhower

Although no one can accurately predict the future, we must not hesitate to say what we expect, and we at Vote World Government think that a global mandate for a "directly-elected, representative, and democratic world government" exists. We think this mandate can be collected (how quickly is partly up to you). If and when it is collected,[128] or *while* it is being collected, a World Electoral Commission should be set up to establish the boundaries of DWG constituencies, settle constituency boundary disputes and plan out the first global DWG general election. In this future election, 700+ MGPs (Members of the Global Parliament, or "representatives"[129]) will be chosen, and an elected, duly-constituted DWG will have been made operational. At that time, humanity, having rejected even the remote *possibility* of omnicide, can get on with the next million years of our life as an intelligent species— as a peaceful, industrious, creative and life-affirming species, to put a finer point on it.

If we can free ourselves from fear and danger for a generation or three, there would likely be very few people left who would even try to promote a "need" to bomb another nation for self-defence. Please accept that central to this plan is the need to stop human-on-human savagery. I would estimate that ninety-nine percent of all people would very strongly prefer to live their entire lives without being attacked and without wanting to attack anyone else out of fear or anger. If we get to this "promised land," I think anyone advocating a return to the literally barbaric circumstances of the early 21st century will be thought of as an unfunny joke, and would be encouraged to seek psychiatric treatment. If we can get to that very good place, and hold on to it tightly for even a few decades, I doubt that anyone will ever again talk with any pride or nostalgia about the "good old days" of overkill nuclear arms races and irreversible or abrupt global warming.

---

[128] Through the Internet effort *or* by national governments running segments of a world referendum *or* by a combination of the two *or* by yet other means.

[129] Again, what they are called hardly matters.

> **There are plenty of problems in the world, many of them interconnected. But there is no problem which compares with this central, universal problem of saving the human race from extinction.** John Foster Dulles, former U.S. secretary of state, speech to the UN General Assembly, 1952

There is an almost endless list of agenda items that the DWG should deal with. But this is not the place to resolve all the debates we can expect to see undertaken once the "writing is on the wall" and the formation of a true DWG is considered not just doable, but inevitable, and even imminent. With regard to the global referendum, we should probably assume that it is going to be up to us ordinary people to finish it, all by ourselves. Then, if governments and companies and newspapers and religions decide to help, that's great (and if they don't help, shame on them).

> **The document** [referring to the 1948 *Declaration of Human Rights*] **represents an important step on the path towards the juridical-political organization of the world community.** Pope John XXIII

Humans have great powers to change things, but if we are to use our freedoms and abilities wisely, we must make a commitment (as doctors do) to "do no harm."[130] Having done that, there is practically no limit at all to the freedom we can enjoy, freedom to say or do or be or believe whatever we please, as long as we do no harm. "Harm" is a general term for what it is we need to get rid of, what we quite rightly fear, and what it is that we were admittedly built by "Nature" to do.[131] But if there is a human instinct to fight and kill, it was appropriate only in the jungle, during that vast stretch of time in which our ancestors had no weapons ... *particularly* no weapons of mass destruction. Nature also gave us big brains and a survival instinct. I suggest we make best use of our outsize brains to size up our situation and do what it takes to survive indefinitely as a species and as a planet.

---

[130] A phrase associated with the "Hippocratic Oath" that must be "taken by all doctors prior to beginning any medical practice, affirming their obligations and proper conduct." (From the *Concise Oxford Dictionary.*) Also, it is commonly (if incorrectly) quoted as: "*First*, do no harm."

[131] I don't mean to insert intentions or directionality into the processes of evolution, but carnivores kill other living animals to eat them, so to survive, and we are carnivores, with all of the same instincts as other carnivores, even though in the developed world at least, the search for food is not too stressful a matter, and usually amounts to nothing more difficult than the occasional walk to a grocery store.

> **Political thinkers are beginning to say ... that the cause of civilization is lost unless nation states will agree to abandon some part of their sovereignty.** Lionel Curtis, *World Order*, Oxford University, 1939

Now that technology is here to stay and our power-to-destroy threatens to overwhelm our power-to-create, we have to begin to live by reason. And if we "feel" that we must express our primitive instincts, we should do that through competitive sports[132] or within the capitalist arena[133] or maybe by participating in partisan politics at national, provincial or local levels.[134]

> **Our ideal is a world community of states which are based on the rule of law and which subordinate their foreign policy activities to law.** Mikhail Gorbachev, in a speech to the UN in 1988

In summary, there is much to be done by everyone, by you and me and by the World Electoral Commission, once it is in place. There are many issues that will surface in the process by which a world constitution is to be written. Yet more issues will await the deliberations of the DWG, once it has been elected and a world constitution has been adopted. No one can predict how all these matters will be resolved. There are mundialist groups that can list the main questions easily enough, and suggest solutions, but the real answers to most of these questions will arise out of the dynamics of the DWG itself, in the centuries and millennia that lie ahead.

I am reasonably optimistic that we can get these things done in time, before a climate change "tipping point" brings us to the tragic moment at which further human intervention will be in vain, when the fate of Earth is sealed and the slide into oblivion is declared unstoppable, and irreversible. I am optimistic, but not very confident. I strongly urge you, everyone, to get involved now, and stay involved for the rest of your life. We don't have any

---

[132] As in "my favourite boxer can beat your favourite boxer," or "my soccer or hockey team can knock the stuffing out of yours with their hands tied behind their backs," etc. There is nothing wrong with sport, even body-contact sport, as long as no serious harm is done and people enjoy themselves.

[133] As in "life is a game and whoever has the most money when they die, wins."

[134] At a global level, it may be best, and perhaps even necessary, to avoid "party" politics, because humanity is, as a whole, a collection of minorities. I don't think party politics would work at the DWG. My view of the ideal MGP would be an honest, intelligent person whose primary interest is the good of the human race and the planet, and whose commitment to any ideology, religion or cultural/ethnic tradition is secondary to that.

guarantee of success, or a certified-reliable roadmap for every issue. What we do have is the wonderful privilege of making a personal decision that helps make all these things happen. And every time a new roadblock pops up, we have to be ready to remove it or to find a way around it.

> **A third Parliament of World Religions convened in Capetown, South Africa, in 1999 and another convened in Barcelona, Spain, in 2004. Key themes discussed in 1999 were: pursuit of world peace, improved environmental stewardship, global sustainability and fair economic practices. Key topics in 2004 were: religious violence, access to safe water, fate of refugees and the elimination of developing countries' debts. Notice that most of the topics discussed in both 1999 and 2004 were not about theology; they were about people and environmental issues.** David E. Christensen, *Healing the World*, page 102

To do all these things, there must emerge some kind of alliance among those who share our goals, and these "allies" must learn to work together. While any example would do, let us start with the one that may well be the trickiest ... religion. (See also Chapter 14 to get a better idea of the kind of cooperation that is needed ... or is at least hoped for.)

> **Mankind's problems can no longer be solved by national governments. What is needed is world government.** Jan Tinbergen, when with the World Bank, *1994 Human Development Report*

Religions do exist, and people believe many different things about the meaning of life and death, and it is historical fact that religious differences are at the root of *many* human conflicts (and I mean the kind where lots of people die pointlessly). Just as we have no plan to blend all cultures into a single soup, or to abandon all languages except English, there is no future in even attempting to get all religions to agree on theological or "spiritual" matters. But I see no reason why all religions cannot agree that they are all trying to do what is right or good, and that killing those we disagree with and destroying our planet through malice or negligence is neither right nor good. So there is the common ground for religion, and I would think that it is enough—enough to be absolutely sure their differences are not allowed to contribute to the overall risks of omnicide ever again, sufficient to serve as a basis for a coordinated effort by and among all our religions to prevent omnicide ... forever.

> **... this planet must to some degree be brought under unified control. Our task, our duty, is to attempt to institute this unified control in a democratic way ...** Emery Reves, *The Anatomy of Peace*, 1945

As it happens, a few years ago I ran into a document by Lewis Browne, written back in 1946, entitled "Mankind's Golden Rule." It is a condensed version of his book, *The World's Great Scriptures*. He lists the same basic message of "love your neighbour as yourself" from seven of the world's great religions, as follows (and using his terminology and spellings):

Brahmanism [now generally called Hinduism]: This is the sum of duty: Do naught unto others which would cause you pain if done to you. *Mahabharata 5:1517*

Buddhism: Hurt not others in ways that you yourself would find hurtful. *Udanavarga 5:18*

Confucianism: Is there one maxim which ought to be acted upon throughout one's whole life? Surely it is the maxim of loving-kindness: Do not unto others what you would not have them do unto you. *Analects 15:23*

Taoism: Regard your neighbor's gain as your own gain, and your neighbor's loss as your own loss. *T'ai-Shang Kan-Ying P'ien*

Judaism: What is hateful to you, do not to your fellow man. That is the entire Law; all the rest is commentary. *Talmud, Shabbat 31a*

Christianity: All things whatsoever ye would that men should do to you, do ye even so to them: for this is the Law and the Prophets. *Bible, New Testament, Matthew 7:12*

Islam: No one of you is a believer until he desires for his brother that which he desires for himself. *Sunan*

> **There is no such thing as a good war or a bad peace.** Benjamin Franklin

I see no reason why these seven religions, and all others, cannot agree that they possess this common ground, and upon that basis, setting aside all differences, they should be able to work together with all other religions, and with non-believers who are equally committed, to save the world from human abuse. To this exhortation I will add one truism that I think would apply here: "If you are not part of the solution, you may well be part of the problem." All religions, corporations and nation states—in fact all groups of people—are going to either help or hurt the campaign to "fully civilize" planet Earth. Our hope is that once this is realized, our list of active allies will grow until our chances of failure are reduced to zero.[135]

> **The terror-filled anaesthesia which numbed rational thought, made nuclear war thinkable and grossly excessive arsenals possible during the Cold War is gradually wearing off. A renewed appreciation for the obscene power of a single nuclear weapon is taking a new hold on our consciousness, as we confront the nightmarish prospect of nuclear terror at the micro level.** General Lee Butler, Former Commander, Strategic Air Command, speech at the State of the World Forum, San Francisco, October 3, 1996

> **I am a citizen, not of Athens, or Greece, but of the World.** Socrates (5th Century BCE)

> **Few will have the greatness to bend history itself, but each of us can work to change a small portion of events, and in the total of all those acts will be written the history of this generation.** Robert F. Kennedy

> **I want to record my strong conviction that the risks entailed by nuclear weapons are far too great to leave the prospects of their elimination solely within the province of [national] governments.** General Lee Butler, Former Commander, Strategic Air Command, speech at the State of the World Forum, San Francisco, October 3, 1996

> **All of us might wish at times that we lived in a more tranquil world, but we don't. And if our times are difficult and perplexing, so are they challenging and filled with opportunity.** Robert F. Kennedy

---

[135] There is a link on our site called "Allies," and while it contains a rather short list at the time of writing (2007), I hope that it will have grown substantially by the time you read this book and check out www.voteworldgovernment.org.

Chapter 9

What about the United Nations?

> **The United Nations is an extremely important and useful institution provided the peoples and governments of the world realize that it is merely a transitional system toward the final goal, which is the establishment of a supranational authority vested with sufficient legislative and executive powers to keep the peace.** Albert Einstein[136]

> **The cure for terrorism lies at its source. Systems like the UN (that second League of Nations) are merely efforts to constitutionalize and legalize world anarchy, attempts to keep the peace by warlike means, which inflict misery on the weak and the innocent while the guilty go untouched. Thus all systems based on national sovereignty are pretending to cure the disease of war without harming the germ that causes it.** Harold S. Bidmead, *Tilting at Windbags: The Autobiography of a World Federalist*

It would be nice to think that national governments could manage world affairs through the UN, but they can't … or won't (the net effect is the same). The UN has done terrific work in the areas of education, health, refugees and more, and if there were a wall of honour to celebrate *avoided* wars, the UN would likely be the only name on that wall. But there is no such wall, and wars continue to happen, and mass killings also continue to happen in ways other than war. Most people don't go through life looking for people to kill or for better ways to do their killing—in fact, most people who get involved in killings are the *victims* of the rather few people who are like that. These few, who are willing to employ armed force to get what they want, *make the rest of us respond*—fight back, or cower in fear, or, worst of all, go along with the violence, become part of it, even if, in our hearts and our minds, we know this is no way for a brilliant species like *Homo sapiens* to behave … *especially* now that the result of war could be omnicide.

So what *about* the United Nations? Should it be scrapped when the DWG is established? Would it be replaced by the DWG?

---

[136] Einstein could have added "judicial" to his list of powers, of course. This was likely nothing more than an oversight (even a genius can have those).

Many views will emerge if and when the achievement of our goal starts to look like a done deal or a very serious probability, but it is reasonable to assume that there will always be an important role for the UN to play in the management of world affairs. It is quite obvious that we must devise daring new institutions suitable for the 21st century and beyond, but we should be careful not to "throw the baby out with the bathwater." If we are going to maintain peace for the rest of human history (which must be our goal), we will need to use every advantage we can get (if only because villains have so many advantages, and we will likely never reach a time when there are no more villains). If some national governments want nothing to do with the DWG, then we, the people of Earth, will just have to "start without them," as writer and social activist George Monbiot has suggested.[137]

It is reasonable to expect that once the DWG is in place, it will link up with the UN.[138] In England, when the House of Commons was created, it had to wrest its powers from the monarch and from the aristocracy. Seven centuries later, although all of the *real* political power resides in the directly-elected House of Commons, there is still a monarch and a House of Lords in the UK, and while some British citizens resent their continued existence, most think that these two institutions still play valued and useful roles.

Most world citizens expect that a DWG will inevitably become a "third house" within the UN structure, although like in the UK, this third house (the commoners' house or the DWG) is intended to have power over the upper houses in a pinch.[139] Without going into too much detail, the UN General Assembly is mainly a meeting place of national governments, the counterpart to the UK's House of Lords. The UN's Security Council is a meeting place of a small group of privileged national governments, and it can be seen (collectively) as the counterpart of a British monarch. It has five permanent member states—Russia, the USA, Britain, France and China—who possess the much-criticized veto power (a special power these nations demanded as the "victors" in WWII), and ten temporary members who

---

[137] *New Internationalist* (Jan/Feb 2002) article entitled "A parliament for the planet." His words: "So, given that nation states will be reluctant to surrender their illegitimate control over global governance, how do we persuade them to make way? The answer, I think, is that we don't. We simply start without them. There are signs that this is happening, organically, already."

[138] This does not mean that the DWG would be physically based in the United States. Indeed, Americans are not expected to be the biggest fans of the DWG (at first), nor would the Members of the Global Parliament be voting en masse to locate there, I wouldn't think. However, modern technology means that there is no real need for the two institutions to be in close physically proximity.

[139] In Canada, we have a system in which the British monarch is represented by a Governor General. Our Canadian Senate is analogous to the UK's House of Lords, and our House of Commons, where elected politicians represent all us "common" people, has, for all practical purposes, all of the *real* power.

don't have veto power.[140] Over the years, the DWG (or global parliament) would have to (and surely will) "earn its stripes," and acquire the power to have the final word on every agenda item in the supranational envelope, based on its valid claim to represent the human race as a whole, even if the two other "houses" continue to play a role, and have a voice, and exert an influence.

Will there always be tensions and disagreements among these various bodies? Yes, of course there will. This is politics, after all, and politics is all about tensions and how they are resolved. If you don't like politics, that's fine, but tensions and competing interests will always exist, and if we don't establish institutions that can and do reconcile and balance out these forces, and do it very well for the rest of human history, then we are back to the threat and use of violence to sort things out, and that simply can't happen any more, for reasons explained earlier.

In the long term, the UN should pass a resolution calling on all nations to conduct their segment of the first DWG general election, and welcome the DWG into the circle of global-governance-type institutions. And all UN ambassadors (and the 190+ national governments that they represent) must understand that the DWG will represent the interests of the human race *as a whole*, and it will act accordingly. And the UN as an institution should help us get the new DWG up and running when and if we get to that point. However, what we should ask of the UN directly in the *short term* are these three things:

1) The General Assembly of the UN should help humanity get the global referendum done by passing a resolution calling on every UN member state to conduct a national referendum (on the establishment of a DWG) in conjunction with its next national election (see draft UN resolution in Appendix #2; we can ignore the fact that some governments will likely never do it, since we can fall back on Internet voting in such cases).

2) UN ambassadors and their staff should help the (pre-DWG) World Electoral Commission make optimal boundary decisions for DWG constituencies within their respective nations.

3) Each UN mission should draw up a list of suggestions with regard to the construction of a world constitution (an effort that should soon be underway—see Chapter 12).

---

[140] It used to be six, and was bumped to ten in 1965. These ten member states are elected to two-year terms by the General Assembly. Decisions of the Security Council require nine affirmative votes, including all of the permanent members, since they have vetoes.

If the UN, in its wisdom, provides these things to those who are working on the DWG, that would be very helpful, and appreciated. If the UN ignores or perhaps tries to block the emergence of the DWG, it is our expectation that the only result will be an unfortunate delay in the time it takes for our plans to be realized. As mentioned above, this is a power play, and the entire human race *really is* the top-of-the-food-chain in terms of sovereignty and authority, and surely all national governments represented in the UN would not want the people of Earth (and particularly the people living in their own nation, as these are the people from whom any national government derives its authority) to turn against the UN, and demand its abolition. Failing to assist in this process would reflect extremely poorly on national governments, and on the UN. Even if most national governments try to ignore the emergence of the DWG, I have no doubt that *some* or our national governments will assist us, *outside* of the framework of the UN if necessary, and they will be remembered kindly by history, and by the people of the Earth, for having done so.

Different groups of species are now going extinct 100 to 1,000 times faster than expected. Scientists expect that species extinction rates of 1,000 times higher than expected will be typical within the next few decades. Stuart Pimm, author of *The world according to Pimm, a scientist audits the Earth*

Violence sometimes may have cleared away obstructions quickly, but it never has proved itself creative. Albert Einstein

---

What we need [to fight climate change] **is comparable to the mobilization** [in Canada] **for World War Two…. People have to realize the enormity and the magnitude of the effort that is going to be needed to turn this around.** Danny Harvey, University of Toronto contributor to the IPCC, *Ottawa Citizen*, November 17, 2007

My pacifism is not based on any intellectual theory but on a deep antipathy to every form of cruelty and hatred. Albert Einstein

Chapter 10

A legally binding mandate?

There are many arguments to support the validity and legality of a global referendum on democratic world government. Nevertheless, the authority or effect of the mandate that would derive from such a planetary effort will no doubt be challenged by many existing powers.

Referendums are ordinarily conducted under the authority of a national, provincial (state) or municipal government, in accordance with laws or resolutions that those various governments enact. Because we are considering a global referendum, and since no global government exists at this time, we cannot claim that kind of authoritative sanction for it. There are, however, many analogous precedents and legal principles to support both the process and the binding effect of such a global referendum.

In past centuries, governments and nations have been created, if not directly by "the people," at least with their basic support or acquiescence. Constitutions creating a higher level of government were written and ratified by the victors in revolutions and wars, or by the leaders of "lesser" states wishing (or forced) to unite to form a much stronger state to defeat an internal or external threat. These founding documents are often not ratified *directly* by the people involved, but gain their credibility and authority indirectly, through subsequent support of their drafters, and/or a willing adherence to their terms by the people affected.

It is not surprising that the founders of nations (or empires) did not provide for global referendums. Their focus was power *within* the nation state. Nor is it surprising that the victors in WWII didn't make provision for global referendums when they met to establish the United Nations. Their stated purposes were, among other things, to prevent all future war, to strengthen human rights and international law and to promote social progress (see the Preamble to the UN *Charter*).

Their "solution" was focused on attempting to eliminate the causes of war between or among nations by establishing *higher but undemocratic* forums, like the UN and its related organs, in which disputes between nations could be resolved while still maintaining the then-existing power bases and confirming the sovereignty and the (artificially-established) borders of all nation states. In theory, individuals were represented by their national government, and they were supposed to be free to work within that framework, without outside interference, to bring about changes they believed necessary for their individual and collective peace and security. It hasn't worked out very well, in large part because national governments predictably sought to maintain or enhance their national power through short-sighted policies, often at the expense of their own citizens and other peoples. Until recently, little thought was given to the fact that the Earth is like a spaceship in which all passengers must rely on the same finite supply of life-sustaining resources and the same destructible ecosystems.[141]

The "victors" of WWII did, however, articulate some important and widely accepted principles that have been expanded and refined by the member states of the UN. In the last 50 years, international law has evolved from a system focused almost exclusively on relations between nations to a system encompassing the rights of individuals as well as the responsibilities of national governments towards their own citizens. These new laws and principles, established or confirmed in numerous international covenants, declarations or treaties, clearly support the legitimacy and binding nature of a global referendum.

In the preface to the *Constitution* of Japan of November 3, 1946, it is stated that:

> We, the Japanese people, acting through our duly elected representatives in the National Diet … do proclaim that **sovereign power resides with the people** and do firmly establish this Constitution. **Government is a sacred trust of the people, the authority for which is derived from the people**, the powers of which are exercised by the representatives of the people, and the benefits of which are enjoyed by the people.… **This is a universal principle of mankind** upon which this Constitution is founded. … we have determined to preserve **our security and existence, trusting in the justice and faith of the peace-loving peoples of the world.** We desire to occupy an honored place in an international society striving for the preservation of peace, and the banishment of tyranny and slavery, oppression and intolerance for all time from the earth. We recognize that **all peoples of the world have the right to live in peace, free from fear and want.** We believe that no nation is responsible to itself alone, but that **laws of political morality are universal; and that obedience to such laws is incumbent upon all nations** who would sustain their own sovereignty and justify their sovereign relationship with other nations.… (Emphasis mine.)

---

[141] British artist and writer Wyndham Lewis wrote that "the earth has become one big village" in his 1948 book *America and Cosmic Man*. Then Lewis's close friend, Canadian Marshall McLuhan, popularized the notion and coined his own expression "the global village" (in his 1962 book *The Gutenberg Galaxy: The Making of Typographic Man*), when it was still considered the conjecture of a quirky egghead. Now the idea of the global village has become an unavoidable observation. Hopefully, we will soon see a sense of "human family" or "sibling loyalty" replace the easily-stirred enmities that are traceable to divisive factors like race, nationality, language, ideology and religion.

While it may be argued that the above words (no doubt authored by the "victors" and echoing the U.S. *Declaration of Independence*) apply only to the Japanese people, they are mirrored in Article 21 of the *Universal Declaration of Human Rights* of Dec. 10, 1948 U.N.G.A. Res. 217A (III) which provides, *inter alia*:

> (3) **The will of the people shall be the basis of the authority of government;** this will shall be expressed in periodic and genuine elections which shall be by universal and equal suffrage [meaning that every adult gets one vote] and shall be held by secret vote **or by equivalent free voting procedures**. (Emphasis mine. I suggest that the global referendum qualifies as an "equivalent free voting procedure.")

The UN proclaimed this *Declaration* (above) as:

> ... a common standard of achievement for all peoples and **all nations**, to the end that **every individual and every organ of society** ... shall ... by progressive measures, national and international ... secure their universal and effective recognition and observance.... (Emphasis mine.)

These principles also find strong support in the *Declaration on the Inadmissibility of Intervention in the Domestic Affairs of States and the Protection of their Independence and Sovereignty*, U.N.G.A. Res. 2131 (XX), Dec. 21, 1965 where in the Preamble it says:

> *Recognizing* that, in fulfilment of the principle of self-determination, the General Assembly, in the *Declaration on the granting of Independence to Colonial Countries and Peoples* contained in resolution 1514 (XV) of 14 Dec., 1960 stated its conviction that **all peoples have an inalienable right to complete freedom**, the exercise of **their** sovereignty ... and that, **by virtue of that right, they freely determine their political status ...** (Emphasis mine.)

The *International Covenant on Economic, Social and Cultural Rights*, (1966), 993 U.N.T.S.[142] 3, Article 1 (1.) states:

> All peoples have the right of self-determination. By virtue of that right they freely determine their political status ...

---

[142] U.N.T.S. 993 is the document number. U.N.T.S. stands for "United Nations Treaty Series."

These words are repeated in Article I of the *International Covenant on Civil and Political Rights* (1966) 999 U.N.T.S. 171, which contains numerous additional provisions including Article 50, which stipulates:

> The provisions of the present *Covenant* shall extend to all parts of federal States without any limitations or exceptions.

While a people's referendum is not specifically provided for, and it may be argued that all of the citations above refer to rights of self-determination within the boundaries of a nation state, it is submitted that that position is untenable. A "universal" right or power, residing in the individual, can't be constrained by national boundaries. It is universally recognized that the "will of the people" is the basis of all political power and authority and, accordingly, it follows that a clear expression of that "will" must be given effect to by all national governments.

There are two unanswered questions remaining concerning the legal effect of the proposed global referendum. The first is whether or not the question or "proposition" on the ballot is clear, and the ballot wording of the global referendum seems crystal clear to us at Vote World Government. The second question is this: Does a positive ("yes") response establish an irrefutable and unequivocal statement of support for the establishment of such a democratic world government? The answer to this key question appears to depend on two things; the total number of votes cast and the percentage of those voting "yes."

If we conducted a global referendum on democratic world government and 3 billion votes were cast,[143] and the "yes" side won by a 99% to 1% landslide,[144] a DWG *would be built* ... there's no question about that. Such a lopsided outcome would constitute a "legally binding mandate," even if the constitution of every nation in the world forbids the recognition of any higher source of law than the nation state. Such a mandate from a global referendum would not only trump all pre-existing law, but would itself *become* law—the first "*world* law," to be precise. It qualifies as a "world law" because it would have been passed *by the people and for the people*, and so differs fundamentally from international law, which is established *by nation states and* (mostly) *for nation states*.

But what if only 93% voted "yes"? Or 89%? Or 76%? Or 65%? Or perhaps 57%? Somewhere in there, between 50% + 1 and 100%, there

---

[143] There are 6.3 billion people in the world at the time of writing (2007), of which about 4.1 billion are adults, so this hypothetical case implies a turnout at the polls of 75% of all eligible voters, an extremely high and most improbable number.

[144] To be precise, I am talking here about the percentages *of those who voted*, and I assume that there would have been sufficient facilities, time, publicity and debate so that all adults had the chance to cast an *informed* vote.

simply has to be a minimum number that works. Less than that, and the DWG may not succeed because it wouldn't have the level of respect (from national governments or corporations *or* ordinary people) needed to *allow* it to work. It is necessary to anticipate that only a *sufficient* show of strength would permit those who voted "no" in the global referendum (and people who still have serious doubts or reservations about the DWG) to accept the global referendum's voting result as a "true expression" of the will of the world's people. There must be a *significant* majority voting in favour for the DWG's authority to be respected enough for its laws to be enforceable. Furthermore, we must be mindful of the unique difficulties involved in a process of this magnitude. We need to make allowances for duplicate votes, ineligible voters *and* for people who had voted and then died (because this referendum may take place over a period of years, the time taken depending on how it is done). The normal standard of 50% + 1 (of all votes cast) would not be sufficient to be generally accepted as reasonable or fair in a global referendum.

Since the lofty purpose of this proposed global referendum is to establish a new order of government with its own charter or constitution, a margin of two thirds (66.7%) of the votes cast by a global turnout of at least half of all the eligible voters would seem a more appropriate standard,[145] especially as that is the exact level of voter support required to change the constitutions of many nations, and since a successful global referendum on DWG may have the effect of requiring changes to the constitutions of most nations (possibly even *all* nations). We also think that national governments cannot legitimately set a higher standard for their people than they have set for themselves. Indeed, national governments should have to operate under the highest standard, since they are in positions of trust.

If and when the number of votes cast for a democratic world government crosses the two billion mark, it [the global mandate] **automatically acquires moral legitimacy and legal sanctity even if not one national government supports it.** Raj Shekhar Chandola, Head of the World Unity and Peace Education Department at City Montessori School in Lucknow, India

---

The problem with this higher standard is that getting 50% of all adults in the world to vote is a daunting task. And getting a 66.7% "yes" vote will

---

[145] If the global referendum were done today, with about 6 billion people in the world, that translates into about 4 billion adults, and a 50% turnout would be 2 billion votes, and 2/3rds of that would be 1.33 billion "yes" votes, the absolute minimum number needed to say that the referendum had "passed."

be no easy job either, since there will inevitably emerge a "no" campaign that will use negative ads to scare people away from voting in favour of something this new and this big. Those promoting the global referendum on DWG are hoping for a strong "yes" vote, but we are also aware that we may not be able to meet this very high standard. Still, we must accept this standard, and we must simply do our best to meet or exceed it.

Assuming the effort is made, and we meet or exceed this high standard, it is satisfying to realize that the whole world would actually *be* something of a democracy then,[146] since it would have been "declared" a democracy by all those who voted "yes" for the creation of the brand new democratic world government.[147] Before the advent of the idea of a global referendum as a credible instrument for democratic, global decision-making there was no mechanism by which billions of people could pool their tiny bits of power in such a way as to lock arms and eventually prevail in the global political marketplace. It will be by virtue of the fact that billions of virtually powerless individuals have indeed voted "yes" that we get to win.[148] The people of planet Earth are *entitled* to make such a decision, and I believe that they (or rather "we") will do exactly that, soon.

However, just guessing at the "magic" combination of numbers doesn't accomplish much. As I mentioned earlier, the alternative to anarchy, or the *antidote* to anarchy, is law. If we are to become "a world of laws," in the same way that democratic countries proudly declare themselves to be "nations of laws," we have to look at what the law *as it exists now* has to say about the power of a mandate that emerges from a referendum.

I set out in 2005 to find a lawyer who would address our basic legal question.[149] The first to do so was a former professor of law hailing from Sri Lanka. (The question of whether or not the mandate from a successful global referendum would have the hoped-for *legal* effect was put to him directly by a friend of mine in India.) He responded: "*Of course* (emphasis

---

[146] Perhaps I should say "the world as a whole," since that can be true even if there are still some national governments that have no respectful regard for the "will of the people" they govern. And if there are still dozens of undemocratic nations in the world, that number will shrink over time if democracy is working above them (at the new DWG) and all around them (within most municipalities, most provinces and most other national governments).

[147] Indeed, arguments will be made that this point has to be taken long before we reach even the *one* billion "yes"-vote mark, if only because people-power has to win the day eventually.

[148] If we had to wait until 98% of a national population voted for democracy in order to make a democracy, there would not be one democratic country in the world today. Bullies and dinosaurs win disputes by killing. Democrats win by argument, and by the numbers— not in opinion polls, but at real voting stations, in real elections, or in a real local, provincial, national or global referendum (or by way of a real vote among the *representatives* of the people who have elected them, from real political constituencies, for membership in the DWG, or any of the other levels of democratic government).

[149] Long and very sad story there … but never mind.

his) a global mandate would be legally binding." However, he declined to expand on what exact numbers might be needed. And he expressed the additional view that it would "never" be possible to conduct such a global referendum or collect such a mandate, matters on which I must respectfully disagree with him.

Our organization didn't have the money to hire a lawyer, but I did find a professor of law in Ottawa (near my home town) who discussed these questions with me over the phone. Following that indecisive encounter, I emailed an old acquaintance from the days of the Cold War, David Wright, a lawyer, now retired. He and I had not been in touch for more than twenty years, but he agreed to research the legal citations and arguments presented above, for which we can be grateful.

The bottom line seems to be that what *current* law has to say about the legal punch of the mandate from a "successful" global referendum is quite favourable ... and most encouraging. However, this question also brings us onto unbroken ground, into virgin territory. While a verified and collected "global mandate" is likely to cause serious problems for any constitutional lawyer who doesn't want the DWG to exist, to ask if a global mandate would be legally binding *in advance of the fact of the collected mandate* may well be to ask a question for which there is, at present, no *definitive* legal answer. So, as the law professor in Ottawa advised, let us then look into the *politics* of this situation.

Perfection of means and confusion of goals seem to characterize our age. If we desire sincerely and passionately the safety, the welfare and the free development of the talents of all men [and women], we shall not be in want of the means to approach such a state. Albert Einstein

---

Nuclear weapons are clearly inhumane weapons in obvious violation of international law. So long as such weapons exist, it is inevitable that the horror of Hiroshima and Nagasaki will be repeated -- somewhere, sometime -- in an unforgivable affront to humanity itself. Takashi Hiraoka, Mayor of Hiroshima, *Hiroshima Peace Declaration*, August 6, 1995

The age of nations has passed. Now, unless we wish to perish, we must shake off our old prejudices and build the earth. Pierre Teilhard de Chardin, 1931 essay, "The Spirit of the Earth"

Chapter 11

A politically binding mandate?

> **If everyone demanded peace instead of another television set, then there would be peace.** John Lennon (who was himself murdered in 1980)

If national sovereignty *is* supreme, and we accept that there can *never* be any "higher" law (except for treaties under international law, in which case there are no real enforcement mechanisms[150]), it would have been pointless to ask the legal question that we asked. But that is not how history unfolds. If the monarchs of the past (some of whom claimed that their power to decide things had been given to them by God in a doctrine known as "the divine right of kings") or the heads of city-states or the warlords of yore had been allowed to prevail when they said that there could never be any higher law than the laws that they decreed for their little fiefdoms, humanity would never have been able to invent or establish the modern nation state … or democracy, for that matter.

Not one national constitution has any provision saying how the nation would respond to a collected and verified mandate from the entire human race for the good reason that no constitutional "framer" in the past would have anticipated such an eventuality. However, if sovereignty "belongs" *not* to any national, provincial or municipal government, but rather belongs to the communities that they serve, then (if democracy has any meaning) we, the people of Earth, have every right to "re-slice the pie," to reassess and change our predecessors' decisions about constitutions, and to do so in such a way as would allow for the emergence of this new "fourth level" of governance. In other words, if our question about the *legal* significance of a strong mandate emerging from a global referendum on DWG can not be *definitively* answered at this time, it is therefore a *political* question, an issue that we now have to address in *political* terms (this of course *in addition to* the legal groundwork presented in Chapter 10, not in place of it).

Long ago—let's say some 25,000 years ago—the name of the game for "hominids" was essentially the same as for all mammals. It was "every man for himself" (or every family group or every tribe for itself). If there had been the word "sovereignty," it would have meant that you as an individual were allowed to do whatever you want or, more to the point, whatever you

---

[150] Well, none that works if one signatory decides to renounce the treaty.

could get away with without getting eaten by a predator or beaten up by one or more of your own species. But somehow—clearly not by voting—every tribe or pack ended up with a leader, and that person's role was to enhance the odds of survival for the whole group. Virtually all leaders were males, and any leader could be ousted in combat by another strong young male (or, presumably, by a hideously strong female) and the tribe as a whole was in no position to disagree with the outcome, or with the process. That is simply how life was for early humans (and it is how life still is for chimps, wolves, and other wild mammals).

In other words, sovereignty was a trait that *belonged to the individual,* or we can say it "resided in the community," and if a particular person became *more* sovereign than all others, it was with the consent (however grudging) of the other members of that group (who still had the option of leaving the group). While the way of choosing a leader may not have been as genteel as one might hope, leadership of a "pack" evolved through a process whereby all of the non-leaders *delegated* aspects of their *individual* sovereignty to the leader (while always reserving the right to challenge the established leader in physical combat and, if one were victorious, to take over the alpha position oneself).

As early humans developed language and tools, the leadership-selection process became a lot more complex, and fairness became an active issue. We invented multitudinous deities[151] to tell us who got to be head honcho (among other things), as would-be leaders tried various ways of becoming leaders and staying in positions of power, even if they were not the biggest or strongest member of the pack, family or tribe. As our species developed agriculture and a few items of technology, larger and larger "tribes" became both possible and necessary, and more and more individual sovereignty had to be delegated from all non-leaders to a leader, or to a leadership group of some kind. And in the same tradition wherein a prey animal is killed and its body is "possessed" by the predator who killed it, chunks of land, territories that were later called nations (or kingdoms or empires), were simply claimed *as if* they were owned by the tribe, this through a monarch (or a chief or a warlord or some such).

The real point of all this is that by whatever means, individuals had to assign a portion of their personal sovereignty—often more than the non-leaders would have liked—to the "leader of the pack," in return for which these "commoners" were supposed to gain a far greater measure of security (and pride, I suppose). As mentioned above, individuals could try to renege

---

[151] It was not my intention here to dismiss all varieties of religious faith, but we should note that no one worships Thor (Norse god of thunder) or Artemis (Greek god of the hunt) any more, or the hundreds or thousands of other deities that have been "believed in" at various times in history, all of which are now universally recognized as human inventions.

on the deal (at the risk of incurring the wrath of the leader), or they could always run off to be a "lone wolf," or to try to join another tribe.

Surprisingly, there is no legal definition for democracy; however, as the weaknesses of all authoritarian systems of governing became obvious, there emerged the new realization that the delegation of a significant part of our individual sovereignty or individual freedom to the leader (or to a leadership group) should be *voluntary*, and *beneficial for all*. One way or another, people developed various forms of democracy, and no one that I'm aware of has ever argued that individuals had no right to voluntarily delegate any portion of their individual sovereignty to a democratic municipal, provincial (state) or national government.[152] If we, the people, fully had this right in the past, we still have the very same right today, and if the existing system enjoyed by a democratic country (generally involving three levels of governance) works well in most respects, we are free, entitled, and, in my view, extremely well advised to delegate *yet another aspect of our personal sovereignty* to a democratic *world* government. Expressed alternatively, we, the people of the Earth, have a *fundamental human right* to delegate the *exercise* of one more aspect of *our* sovereignty to a democratic world government, if that is what we deem to be in our self-interest.[153]

> **In this great nation** [the USA] **there is but one order, that of the people, whose power, by a peculiarly happy improvement of the representative principle, is transferred from them, without impairing in the slightest degree their sovereignty, to bodies of their own creation, and to persons elected by themselves, in the full extent necessary for the purposes of free, enlightened, and efficient government.** Former U.S. president James Monroe (1758-1831)

The distinction between *surrendering* aspects or elements of our personal sovereignty and *delegating* them is important. People do things that are in their own interest, and that is quite normal, and inevitable. When humans delegate *some* of their individual sovereignty to a municipal government, it is

---

[152] This is not a new idea at all. As Eric Schultz wrote (in an article entitled, "What is a world citizen?") "... the Enlightenment philosophers, who created many of our modern concepts of government, stated emphatically that the authority to rule—or 'sovereignty'—is held by the individual citizens, who [can] delegate powers to governments in order to serve their [own] interests." My favourite articulation of this concept is that of Emery Reves in Chapter VIII of *The Anatomy of Peace*, entitled "The historical meaning of sovereignty."

[153] In a democracy, the party in power does not *own* the government, of course, but it is authorized to "run" the government until or unless the people decide otherwise, and in periodic elections, the voters get to decide to keep the party in power for another term, or replace it. We, the people, "own" the government.

not a loss. Indeed, it is a gigantic net gain, and if we disbanded city council tomorrow, we would simply have to reinvent it, if only to re-establish the advantages it offered (garbage pick-up, public parks, snow removal, public libraries, policing, sewage systems, water delivery, some social services, and an economic environment suitable to companies that employ some of the people in our area, etc.).

Similarly, if we were foolish enough to disband the government of our nation tomorrow, we would have to reinvent it, too, in order to regain the valued advantages of our previous life situation, and rather than seeing this reinvention process as any "loss," we would know in advance (from our past experience) that it would be a tremendous bargain, a huge net gain for all.[154] And so, although we have never had a democratic *world* government in the past, we can know by way of analogy that the process of authorizing and establishing a DWG is not to be seen as the loss of something dear to us, but probably as the best bargain we have ever struck, in virtually every sense, with a net gain that dwarfs whatever loss or cost there may be. And if these *four* layers of government (municipal, provincial, national and global) can manage to stay the heck out of each other's jurisdictions, it is entirely possible that the future of humanity and of the Earth will unfold peacefully, allowing us to live and prosper for many millions of years, or perhaps even millions of *generations*, into the future.[155] And now that we know we have the ability and the right to do all this, I fully expect that we will do it.

> **There is an emerging second superpower, but it is not a nation. Instead, it is a new form of international player, constituted by the "will of the people" in a global social movement.** James F. Moore, *The Second Superpower, Extreme Democracy*

Humanity is free to authorize yet another "layer" of governance, and a positive vote from a global referendum would be the obvious and the most democratic way to legally authorize such a choice.[156] If we get a good result (say at least 50% of adults vote and 66.7% of those vote "yes"), stopping

---

[154] As compared to the anarchy or the chaos that would reign in the absence of a national government.

[155] In science fiction, of course, one often bumps into a 5th level of governance, but that assumes there are intelligent and sentient beings on other planets, and that we will all get around to governing the universe before we destroy it with intergalactic wars.

[156] There are some things that are not appropriately decided by referendums. For instance, one should not decide an issue of minority rights by referendum for the good reason that minorities have rights whether the majority wants them to have those rights or not. If we decided such issues by referendum, that would fall into the category of the "tyranny of the majority."

that much momentum would be impossible, or at least *very* difficult. Who is politically able to tell the entire human race that the thing they voted for can never be allowed to happen? No person or nation or even *group* of nations could say that and make it stick. Some parties may try and stop us, but if we represent the human race, the question arises, who do *they* represent?

The meaning of democracy is continuously being refined and redefined by the actions of democratic governments.[157] Democratic legislatures pass laws on a wide range of issues, laws that are not specifically intended to define what a democracy *is*, but which, in the end, have that effect. In my country of Canada, an interesting example of this process emerged only a few years ago.

One province, Québec, is largely French-speaking, while the rest of the nation is largely English-speaking. In the 1970s, some of those who wanted Québec to be an independent French-speaking country resorted to violence (they put bombs inside mailboxes and kidnapped and murdered a British diplomat, among other things). The situation was seen as being so grave that then-prime minister Pierre Trudeau temporarily suspended all our civil rights (which he was legally entitled to do under the old but rarely-used *War Measures Act*[158]) in order to deal with the "uprising."

Eventually, things became quiet again. The separatists decided to settle the issue in a referendum, a *provincial* referendum. They formed a separatist political party (the Parti Québécois, or PQ) which then won the provincial legislature, and conducted such a referendum in 1980, and a second one in 1995.[159] Both these referendums failed to win a majority for the separation option, but they failed only by very slim margins. The "no" side won by 59.6% to 40.4% in the first referendum, and by only 50.6% to 49.4% in the second. Not too surprisingly, the government of Canada was in full panic mode after the 1995 referendum, having "almost lost the country" (as it was at that time expressed).[160]

---

[157] And courts … but that's a long discussion.

[158] See http://www2.marianopolis.edu/quebechistory/readings/warmeas.htm for more. The *Act* came into being in 1914, and was used only twice (in 1939, just as WWII began, and again in 1970). Article 6 (5) reads: "The protection and guarantees extended to Canadians by the Canadian Bill of Rights, and other Charters of Rights in operation provincially in Canada, are waved aside while the *Proclamation* (of the *War Measures Act*) is in effect."

[159] Giving rise to the new expression in Canada, the "never-endum referendum," meaning that the separatists in Québec will just keep holding referendums until one passes, and then they will get what they want.

[160] In the late 1990s, the Liberal government of Jean Chrétien threw so much money at Québec-based Liberal advertising firms (to promote Canada) that a $100-million mess, later dubbed the Sponsorship Scandal, emerged (which further exacerbated relations between English and French Canada).

Canada's constitution, the *British North America Act*, or *BNA Act*, has no provisions for the secession of a province from Confederation.[161] The government of Canada could not answer the key question of what it would do if there were a third Québec referendum that *passed*, especially if the proposition on the ballot was unclear, or the margin of the victory for the separation option was razor thin. So the federal government properly sent the matter to the Supreme Court as a "reference," a plea for guidance. The Justices said that if the question on the ballot was clear and if the majority of "yes" votes was substantial, the government of Canada would have (in their words) "a political obligation" to negotiate fair terms of secession with the province of Québec. As a result of this reference, the government of Canada enacted the *Clarity Act*, formalizing this new state of affairs.[162]

The point here is that the "will of the people" was recognized by the Supreme Court as the final word on this matter (provided the question on the ballot was clear, etc.). It can be cogently argued that the Court did little more than "make virtue of necessity." If the Supreme Court Justices had made a determination that the province of Québec had *no* right to secede just because that eventuality was not thought of when the *BNA Act* was written, that would have forced separatists to either abandon their dream (which is most improbable) or, more likely, revert to the threat and the use of violence to try to get what they wanted, meaning a right and ability to govern themselves as a nation, the right of "self-determination," to which they *feel* they are entitled.[163]

But what the Supreme Court of Canada *actually* did, as I see it, was to *help define what democracy means*, and it means that *at the end of the day, the will of the people matters most*. And if the will of the people of *one province* must be allowed to essentially trump the constitution of the Canadian nation and the obvious will of the other three-quarters of the population of Canada, it is not radical in the least to suggest that *the will of the entire human race must be deemed to trump the constitution of Canada or the constitutions of all countries*, and trump all national, provincial and municipal laws that may be found to be in conflict with *world* law.[164] To say it more plainly, in the event of a conflict between a particular *world* law and any lower-body law, *it is world law that must*

---

[161] In democratic law, where there is silence, the rights involved are reserved by the people.

[162] For more information, go to www.canadianlawsite.com/clarity-act.htm

[163] The whole question of *feeling* entitled as opposed to *being* entitled in law is a matter I do not have time to discuss here. Suffice it to say that human beings do have feelings, and we ignore them at our peril, even if another person's feelings may seem irrational or wrong to us.

[164] In the same way that national laws must and do trump all our provincial and municipal laws, and provincial laws trump municipal laws. All this "trumping" refers only to situations where the law at one level conflicts with law at another level, which happens rather rarely among the three layers of law that now exist (in most democratic countries).

prevail (although there is always a place for compromise in a democratic political process), not precisely *or even mainly* for legal reasons, but because *politically*, any other approach would almost certainly self-destruct in time. (I can't "prove" that last bit, but it is my opinion, and my reading of history.)

> **With all my heart I believe that the world's present system of sovereign nations can only lead to barbarism, war and inhumanity, and that only World law can assure progress towards a civilized, peaceful community.** Albert Einstein

If the DWG, for instance, says that Canada is producing far too many greenhouse gases that threaten the life-support system of the planet as a whole, and a Canadian prime minister insists that our national government has set its own limits and explains that we are well within those limits, Canada can and should be *legally obliged* to comply with world law or risk the imposition of some economic sanctions or other types of pressure from the global community, through the world parliament. Just as I have no right to blow up my neighbourhood, a nation has no right to destroy or to seriously harm the world as a whole, and in the same way that it takes our national, provincial and local law (and law enforcement) to assure that no individual endangers his or her neighbourhood, it is going to take enforceable world law to assure that no nation or group of nations will make life miserable or dangerous for the populations of the other countries, provinces and cities that exist in the same world.

In short, if the French-speaking minority that is living in Canada can be considered "a people," or if other national populations or ethnic groups or language groups can be deemed to be "peoples," and if the main concern with this label ("a people") is that too *small* a group may claim to be "a people," then we can surely assert with passion, if not with legal authority, that the human race *as such* is "a people," and is therefore entitled, like any other "people," to full relief from a very destructive system of 194 "national sovereignties."[165] If the human race is "a people" in the legal definition of the term (and I cannot see why such an assertion wouldn't hold up), then it

---

[165] As an aside, it is my view (as laid out in my 2nd *LieDeck* novel) that if we do manage to establish a DWG, the number of nations in the world will increase, as all national borders would increasingly match up with ethnic and/or language perimeters. Personally, I would rather see my own country of Canada remain as it is, but by this theory, the chances of Québec separation are increased with the full arrival of a warless world of law. A similar speculation can be made in regard to the many other separatist movements that exist within countries around the world. All national borders were created by force, or at a time when violence and/or the threat of violence was a mainstay of international or "inter-people" dealings; thus, they are all open to review or reconsideration in a warless world of law.

can be argued cogently that the human race is *legally entitled* to govern itself globally.[166] That is a right I claim, a *human right* that I think all people really do have, and should now claim, out loud. And if this legal basis is rejected, we can still fall back on the politics of the situation as described above— complete the global referendum, then dare anyone to tell the entire human race to get stuffed. (It will be rather interesting if a court of law must assess the import of the mandate from a successful global referendum.)

We prefer world law in the age of self-determination to world war in the age of mass extermination. John F. Kennedy, in a speech to the UN General Assembly, 1961

Still, whatever the verdicts legally and politically, people will worry that a democratic world government could and may push national governments around, even assuming that the principle of subsidiarity[167] is in full play at the DWG. This worry is not an idle concern, but the human future without the DWG will be *infinitely* worse than a mere political dispute between levels of government.

No national law, no national precautions, can save the planet. Thor Heyerdahl, Norwegian ethnographer and adventurer, famous for his Kon-Tiki Expedition

---

In the 1990s, three scientists basically saved the world[168] from a disaster due to ozone depletion by discovering that the problem was being caused by human-made chemicals, CFCs. Tim Flannery writes that it was nothing but good old "dumb luck that our world did not enter a far more severe environmental crisis, perhaps leading to the collapse of societies ... thirty years ago."[169] He explains that: "This [collapse] could have occurred if [our

---

[166] In my phone chat with the Ottawa lawyer (mentioned in Chapter 10), he said that this principle (that a people is entitled to self-determination) "... is considered part of customary international law, but it's also found in the *UN Charter*, in the *International Covenant on Civil and Political Rights* and in the *International Covenant on Economic, Social and Cultural Rights*."

[167] For those who forgot, this means that all issues ought to be resolved by the "smallest appropriate political unit," meaning the DWG should stay away from issues that can be handled well enough by our nations or provinces or cities.

[168] Paul Crutzen, F. Sherwood Rowland and Mario Molina were jointly awarded the 1995 Nobel Prize in Chemistry for this achievement. (Thanks, guys.)

[169] *The Weather Makers*, page 217. One of the scientists who won the Nobel Prize, Sherwood Rowland, was so struck by the significance of their findings that he said: "I came home one

industries] had used bromine instead of chlorine." These two chemicals are pretty much interchangeable for many purposes, apparently, but bromine is "forty-five times more effective at destroying ozone than chlorine."

We dodged a bullet on that one, but dodging bullets is no way to live, and many other environmental threats abound, particularly climate change. If we can't rely on scientific predictions and/or our rationality to do what needs to be done, some day the human race will have a horrid awakening to the fact that for a century, we have been committing ecocide, and that we do not have the global political institutions needed to bring this horrifying situation under control before the damage becomes irreversible … and our extinction becomes a certainty. Some people argue that it is already too late, but that doesn't help, and it is not supported by facts. (There may be some presently-unknown facts that can change the final verdict, of course.[170])

If that awakening happens in 2040, and the point of irreversible and fatal damage is expected in 2050, and it takes us 25 years to get our act together and create a democratic world body to cope with our mess, what does that mean? It means that we are too late for democracy, and that we will have to create what Tim Flannery calls a "carbon dictatorship," an *un*democratic institution that will wield power globally *without reference to what people might feel or think—about anything*. He gives this body the title of "Earth Commission for Thermostatic Control," and he admits that it could be, *of necessity*, "an Orwellian-style world government with its own currency, army and control over every person and every inch of our planet."[171] That does not sound particularly inviting, but arguably, it beats the alternative—an environmental collapse where Earth becomes inhospitable to mammalian life, or a "protracted Dark Ages far more mordant than any that has gone before."[172] Flannery realizes that the powers of an Earth Commission for Thermostatic Control would inevitably impinge on and clash with national sovereignty, and it is even possible that such a Commission could become the *cause* of wars, become a body that would be obliged to *use* military power against any nation that refused to accept its share of the burden of saving the life-support system of our planet from human devastation.

---

night and told my wife, 'The work is going very well but it looks like the end of the world.'" *The Weather Makers*, page 215.

[170] For a worst-case scenario, see article posted Oct. 17, 2007 at www.rollingstone.com: "The Prophet of Climate Change: James Lovelock"—"One of the most eminent scientists of our time says that global warming is irreversible—and that more than 6 billion people will perish by the end of the century." In a *Scientific American* article (November 26, 2007), "State of the Science: Beyond the Worst Case Climate Change Scenario," climatologist Stephen Schneider, an IPCC "lead author," says we are "25 years too late … to avoid *dangerous* climate change…. The object now is to avoid *really dangerous* [climate] change." (Emphasis mine.)

[171] *The Weather Makers*, Tim Flannery, page 294.

[172] *The Weather Makers*, Tim Flannery, page 291.

> **Population and environmental problems created by non-sustainable resource use will ultimately get solved ... if not by pleasant means ... then by unpleasant ones.** Thomas Malthus, 18th-century philosopher

In Flannery's view, "Humans have come such a very long way in such a brief time that our imaginations are irretrievably mired in the past." It is a brilliant insight, but the word "irretrievably" seems needlessly defeatist. Let us hope that we get our imaginations un-mired from the past in time to deal with our global crisis *democratically*, through a *DWG*, because *the option of not dealing with it isn't even open to us* ... and the non-democratic option may well backfire in the event that we are forced by circumstances to try to repair the Earth that way.[173] As a final nod to the genius that is Tim Flannery, I offer this remarkable quote (pages 294-295 of *The Weather Makers*):

> The Founding Fathers [of the USA] created ... a political entity [a federal government] of sufficient mass to meet the challenges at hand, yet with sufficient safeguards to allow liberty to flourish.... The only way [for the world] to avoid both tyranny and destruction is to act as America's Founding Fathers did ... by ceding just enough power to a higher authority to combat the threat.

I have a great admiration for Tim Flannery, but I worry that he, too, may be a victim of this interesting phenomenon where we seem to get our imaginations "mired in the past."[174] He speaks of the "<u>ceding</u>" of power or sovereignty from nation states to a supranational political entity. I repeat my earlier insistence on an alternative perceptual start point, meaning the idea of *individuals* (alone or viewed as a community) <u>*delegating*</u> the <u>*exercise*</u> of <u>*aspects*</u> of <u>*our*</u> sovereignty to the DWG. This may seem like mere semantics to some people, but I think these distinctions are extremely important if we are to understand what it is, precisely, that we must do, and how we should view this political transformation. (I expect this more accurate perspective will also be important to those brave souls who, in the future, accept the job of "selling" a DWG package to a species that seems to fear the unknown long after all reason and/or science have overcome the expressed bases for such fears.)

---

[173] Interestingly (to me, anyway), I wrote a song called "20th Century Mean" in 1980, more than a quarter century ago, the lyrics of which spoke of a need for a "Big Repair," referring to a "rescue mission," a reversal of the wreckage that we "rational" humans have delivered to planet Earth and to our shared environment.

[174] We all have moments when we catch ourselves burying our heads in the sand like an ostrich, don't we? I know I do.

Imagination is more important than knowledge. Albert Einstein

---

As I mentioned in Chapter 7, once the collective security arrangement of a DWG is in place and working, the money saved from defence budgets by national governments will likely be *much* greater than the financial cost of that collective security apparatus. Let us now look at whatever non-money "costs" may be associated with the establishment of a DWG ... what it is that we will have to give or pay in order to get what we need.

If a referendum proposition for the separation of a substantial part of any political union passes strongly in the province or the region where such an aspiration is expressed, a democratic nation such as Canada *should* find itself morally, politically and (now) legally obliged to negotiate the terms of that separation. In the case of Canada's loss of the province of Québec, the country (well ... the country *as it used to be*) would lose about a sixth of its geography plus about a quarter of its population. However, the addition of a DWG to the global political landscape would not in itself result in *any* loss of land or people by *any* nation. The only things that would be given up are the right to make war on any other nations (or on the citizens of one's own nation) plus the right to ravage the planet by polluting or otherwise harming the environment. These rights must be denied to all people, to all levels of government and to all other human enterprises and groups. In fact these would be two founding principles on which we must build a sustainable, democratized and governed world, meaning a fully civilized world. There must be no murder of any kind,[175] and no trashing of the environment. No homicide, and no ecocide.[176] (And we could learn to "play nice," as well.)

There is another truth that needs to be mentioned. If the human race is no longer losing millions of people every year to genocide, war, starvation, epidemics or medically-preventable deaths,[177] the rate of population growth will *increase* with the establishment of a DWG. To counter this increase *and* reach zero population growth (ZPG) *and* move on from there to population *reduction*, the DWG will surely have to implement effective global programs for population control.

---

[175] It is amazing how many categories of murder there are—homicide, genocide, fratricide, regicide, matricide, patricide, infanticide, and now, of course, the new granddaddy of them all, omnicide—the killing of everyone.

[176] There would still be some pollution, of course, but that would be controlled, diminished according to a timetable, and coordinated with other programs like population reduction. I must emphasize that these are not wild dreams or idealistic speculations, but actions that are *required* of us if life on Earth is to endure indefinitely.

[177] The DWG must see to it that all these bitter tragedies are prevented if it is to represent the interests of the human race as a whole.

Flannery labels overpopulation the "root cause of the issue."[178] And he goes on to say that the single item which could "tip" an Earth Commission on Thermostatic Control from its original design for good geo-engineering projects (like the sequestration of carbon dioxide) over to Big Brother-type, militarily-imposed, interventionist activities will likely be the obvious and unavoidable need to reduce our numbers.[179] The Earth is simply not able to support its *present* numbers of people sustainably, and my guess would be that the ideal number of humans for a *sustainable* planet Earth is under one billion. So, in addition to the removal of the right to kill other people and the right to ravage the planet, we humans will also have to give up our claimed right to reproduce at will (or our *freedom* to reproduce at will), since that is just one more road to chaos and death.

Exactly how we manage to reduce our numbers (other than the use of incentives and disincentives, plus education) is not for me to say. However, if voluntary restraints are recommended by a DWG and are working in general, immigration policy could be used as a further "pressure" on those national governments whose populations continue to grow beyond ZPG (zero population growth). Bear in mind that limiting your number of kids is not *remotely* in the same league as losing your life, which millions of people have been willing to do for their nation since forever. And bear in mind, too, that "world citizenship" will (I hope and truly expect) one day be as important to individual human beings as their national identity is today.

The mention of population control or reduction raises great fears and upsets some of the world's religions. I have been harshly warned that even *mentioning* this issue could damage the prospects of success for the global referendum, and earn me the enmity of powerful and dangerous forces.[180]

There is one alternative (albeit a temporary one) to outright population reduction, and it goes like this. If *all* people living in *all* developed countries consumed *far* less than they do now, humanity would be all right ... at least for a little while longer. The *New Internationalist* (November, 2006) points out that if every person consumed materials and energy like the average American, it would take 5.3 Earths to support the 6.3 billion people who

---

[178] Researcher David Pimentel of Cornell University has deduced that 40 percent of deaths worldwide are caused by water, air and soil pollution (article available at http://www.world-science.net/othernews/070814_disease.htm). He has many devastating figures, such as: "Of the world population of about 6.5 billion, 57 percent is malnourished, compared with 20 percent of a world population of 2.5 billion in 1950." In his view: "Relying on increasing diseases and malnutrition to limit human numbers in the world diminishes the quality of life for all humans and is a high-risk policy." (Such cruelty to mere *animals* would be a crime!)

[179] *The Weather Makers*, page 294.

[180] I respond very poorly to threats. If something important needs to be said, I will say it. The threat and use of force is what we have to get past, and we can't decline to say what needs saying because we are afraid of those who don't want to commit to non-violence.

are now alive. If we all consumed at the rate of the average citizen of China, it would take only two thirds of one Earth to support all of us. And if we all consumed at the rate of the average citizen of India, half an Earth would do the job.

This analysis implies that the problem is not too many people, but too much greed, especially in the developed countries. But this conclusion has some fatal difficulties. First, it is just not credible to suggest that those who live in developed nations will ever *willingly* reduce their standard of living to that of a Chinese or Indian citizen (or anywhere *close* to that). And second, in the unlikely event that we did "even out" the consumption imbalance, population growth would continue, and we will once again be up against the problem of having not-enough-of-everything when we are 10 or 12 billion. If all rich or well-off people want to share with the world's poor (which is *at least* half of humanity), I'm all for that, but even those with religious beliefs saying they *have* to do this type of caring and sharing don't do much of it— *not nearly* enough to make a serious difference. And again, even if they did, if we don't slow down our rate of reproduction, we will only postpone the hardest decisions for a few decades. It is mathematically impossible to get away from the conclusion that we have to at least *stop the net increase* in human numbers, or we will end up with 15 or 20 billion people, at which point nothing short of constant warfare (for increasingly scarce resources) will assure that anyone lives *any* kind of life.

I challenge any theologian or ethicist to justify a reproductive free-for-all that is *mathematically guaranteed* to result in war and chaos and death for hundreds of millions of innocent people … if not the entire human race. Those with religious beliefs that forbid any restriction on the number of offspring will just have to find a new way to cope, either by qualifying the belief or by arranging a kind of "reproductive rights trade" with a couple that cannot have children, or chooses not to have children (a bit like the "Carbon Credits" that are purchased and sold under the Kyoto accord). China's meteoric rise as a place of huge development and wealth has a lot to do with government-set reproductive policies that have the intent and the effect of creating *at least* zero population growth within China's borders.[181] The world needs to find a humane, acceptable system that will produce *at least* ZPG globally, because the alternative is *not* the status quo; the actual alternative would be a coercive system that somehow *forces* the fertility rate down, and surely no one wants that.

The Earth is going to have global governance if the human race is to survive the 21st century. The choice that confronts us now, *a choice we may not have in the future*, is whether we will build a *very democratic* body for world

---

[181] See http://www.uwmc.uwc.edu/geography/Demotrans/irnhnd.htm for more on China's one child policy.

governance or a "Big Brother" kind of institution that will try to save our skins in spite of ourselves. So, let us now return to the question of how law emerged, and see what hope there might be that through world law, we can achieve a much greater real security while at the same time preserving all of the rights and freedoms that can be preserved.[182]

Over large expanses of time, humans tried to minimize chaos in order to allow many other things to flourish, such as commerce, education, sport, travel, family life and art. Since we all have more wants than can ever be filled, and since disagreement constitutes a permanent state of affairs in human society, the basic contest was between two alternative methods of resolving disputes—the rule of force and the rule of law. The big problem is that those who lose in a court of law can resort to using force, or try to, and our history is written in terms of victories and defeats for the advocates of "full civilization"—by which I mean a state of affairs, both legal and real, where violence is absolutely not permitted as a means of resolving disputes (except non-lethally through sport, on the playing field). In the arts, my favourite scene on this item comes from the movie *Camelot*, where King Arthur tries (and fails) to convince a crusty old knight (Pellinore) that laws and courtrooms are far better than bloodshed as the way to resolve all our disputes (see Appendix #4). The same arguments used by this ridiculous knight will likely be resurrected and dusted off in the coming debate about our legal and political efforts to replace war with world law (which requires a world government—hopefully a very democratic one). In the end, human survival likely rides on the success, in this debate, of the side that advocates DWG and world law.

Peace is a product of law and order; law is essential if the force of arms is not to rule the world. Former U.S. Supreme Court Justice William O. Douglas

---

It is important to realize that in many respects, we *already have* world government. The problem is that the global agencies that perform functions that really *ought* to be the responsibility and the job of a DWG—the World Trade Organization, the World Bank, the International Monetary Fund and the UN—are not democratic at present ... nor do they even *pretend* to be democratic ... nor are they ever likely or expected to become democratic through any process of internal reform.[183]

---

[182] Perhaps we may even add *new* rights and freedoms, if and as they are needed and possible, through the DWG.

[183] Hence the emergence of and the need for a world democracy movement.

> **We have been warned by the power of modern weapons that peace may be the only climate possible for human life itself. There must be [democratic] law, steadily invoked and respected, because without law, the world promises only such meagre justice as the pity of the strong upon the weak.** Dwight D. Eisenhower

Carl Nyberg wrote an article entitled: "World government? We already have world government."[184] It begins:

> Before one can decide if world government is good or bad, it is necessary to define what world government is. If government is the institution that governs society, it seems self-evident that we already have world government. We don't have democracy. And we don't have a legislature. But plenty of governments throughout history haven't been democratically accountable to the citizenry. And legislatures are also optional.

He goes on to explain that:

> The World Trade Organization has rules that get enforced through a judicial process. Effectively the rules supersede national law. The WTO is a theocratic oligarchy with a theology which holds that an economic system [capitalism] is the supreme being of the universe.

We can discuss such matters until the cows come home and not resolve much, so I will end this chapter with just two more short items. The first is a comment about the often-curious relationship between law and politics.

In 1983, Operation Dismantle went to court[185] to see if we could stop the testing of American cruise missiles over Canadian territory (we thought we might be able to do this on constitutional grounds). *Based on the law* (or, more precisely, on the law as expressed in the *Charter of Rights and Freedoms* which, in 1981, had recently become a new part of Canada's constitution), I think we should have won that case, but in the end, we lost.[186]

---

[184] *Journal of Oak Park and River Forest*, December 13, 2005.

[185] The first action was in the Federal Court, where we won. The government appealed to the Federal Court of Appeal, where we lost. Then we appealed to the Supreme Court of Canada, where we lost again.

[186] We won in the sense that we established that cabinet decisions were indeed "justiciable" (subject to judicial review), as we had claimed under the then-new *Charter of Rights and Freedoms*, but we lost in the sense that we were not allowed to challenge this *particular* cabinet decision in court (various judges gave differing reasons for the same conclusion). For more on this *Charter* case, go to http://scc.lexum.umontreal.ca/en/1985/1985rcs1-441/1985rcs1-441.html or read Chapter 9 of *Cold War Blues*.

Also in the early 1980s, Operation Dismantle asked a thousand or so Canadian municipalities to run local referendums on balanced and verifiable nuclear disarmament, and when 200 cities and towns agreed to do so, the legal right of cities and towns to do it was challenged in the Supreme Courts of four provinces. *On the law,* we probably should have lost all four of these cases ... but we won them all.

Bottom line? There is a strange nexus of law and politics that lawyers in particular don't like to talk about. In my view, we lost the case we should have won because all the political implications of our winning, or the optics, were wrong.[187] And we won the four cases that we likely should have lost because the politics and optics of those cases were delicious, at least from our point of view.[188] (The full stories of all these legal cases are in *Cold War Blues,* which is now available free online.[189]) With regard to the mandate from a successful global referendum for the establishment of a DWG, as the so-called war on terror drags on, and as alarm over the full impact of climate change grows, the politics and optics of what we are trying to do just keep getting better and better. I hope we are all believers in law, but we must also believe that a smart, aggressive political campaign has to be part of what we do if we are ever to "save the world," as Céline Dion put it.

> **The international community should support a system of laws to regularize international relations and maintain the peace in the same manner that law governs national order.** Pope John Paul II

And finally, this. Along the lines of our (1980s) legal argument about how cities are the main targets of nuclear missiles (and thus are entitled to conduct referendums intended to generate pressure to eliminate nuclear weapons), we can say unequivocally that *there are no human rights whatsoever if there is no prior right of humanity to exist on this planet indefinitely* (or at least until

---

[187] The government was loathe to have this cabinet decision reversed by a mere citizens' group, especially with the U.S. breathing down the PM's neck to get the cruise missile testing done, and arguing (quite spuriously) that it was our duty as a partner in NATO to test the missile. It was recently learned that the government of Canada was so "shaken" by domestic opposition to cruise missile testing that it drew up a list of 2,500 "dissidents" (including me, I have no doubt at all) that it planned to *lock up in internment camps* at any time of "crisis." (*Just Dummies: Cruise Missile Testing in Canada,* by Cold War historian John Clearwater.)

[188] The rulings in these four cases were all slightly different, but the common thread seemed to be "what's the harm," and the scary result of a court ruling *against* us was that dozens of municipal elections might be overturned later, at a cost of many millions of dollars, because some mayors had announced that they were going to hold the referendum even if the courts said they couldn't legally do it!

[189] Go to www.voteworldgovernment.org, and click on the "Books" link. (*Cold War Blues* is also available in hardcover.)

the sun goes supernova, or we get wiped out by an asteroid[190]). Assuming *and asserting* that there exists a prior human right for us to live here,[191] does that right extend to a subsequent right to choose, in a fair referendum, to govern ourselves globally, democratically? Common sense and this claimed and self-evident human right (for us to live on the Earth indefinitely) mean *exactly* that, and thus it can be concluded that world law, meaning all of the legislation that emerges from the DWG, *must* trump all other law when and if there is a conflict between world law and any other body of law, including any national constitutions that may, as they now stand, serve to discourage or to prevent the creation of the DWG, or serve to deny the legitimacy of the DWG's legislative product.

If we reach a point in time where it can be shown that virtually all adults on the Earth have had the opportunity to cast an informed vote in the global referendum on the critical issue of creating a democratic world government, a "yes" result of 66.7% or more simply *has* to be accepted as a *politically* binding mandate, if only because billions of reasonable people will agree and insist that it is so. World law, while it certainly must confine itself to matters that are global or supranational in scope, has to be accepted as both *politically and legally* binding on all individuals, all municipal councils, all provincial (or "state," in the United States) governments, and on all national governments, if only because we, the people of planet Earth (or *most* of us), say so.

Now that the world has shrunk to the point where so many issues *are* global in scope, and some global issues might, if not resolved in the very near future, lead to the extermination of human life and possibly *all* life on Earth, the law itself must adapt to the new material and political conditions of the planet. And if this book has the intended effect, and if you do your part, the political conditions will soon be such that we, the people of the Earth, have already conducted the global referendum on democratic world government, and if we managed to end up with a powerful global mandate, as we fully expect will be the case, we must then construct that institution, a democratic world government, as quickly and well as we can.

Here is a question. Could we start on all those non-referendum-related aspects of the campaign even before the global referendum is done? Well, we should do that, if only to avoid a bottleneck later on. We should do that mainly because our sense of urgency is a key factor, and the *appropriateness* of our sense of urgency will certainly be respected or condemned by all future generations. As I explained earlier, *we are in a true planetary crisis*,[192] whether

---

[190] It is said, accurately, that humans inhabit Earth "by geological permission."

[191] If only because we "found ourselves" here, and are not here as the result of a conscious decision to be here, which are reasons enough to claim this right.

[192] To paraphrase Al Gore's expression, "a true planetary emergency."

we recognize it or not. The rational choice is to confront the problems that confront us … vigorously … and immediately.

Almost imperceptibly, over the last four decades, every nation and every human being has lost ultimate control over their own life and death. For all of us, it is a small group of men and machines in cities far away who can decide our fate. Every day we remain alive is a day of grace as if mankind as a whole were a prisoner in the death cell awaiting the uncertain moment of execution. And like every innocent defendant, we refuse to believe that the execution will ever take place. Members of the Five Continent Peace Initiative, Argentina, India, Mexico, Tanzania, Sweden, and Greece, *The Delhi Declaration*, January 28, 1985

The proposal for a global referendum on democratic world government offers a desperately-needed opportunity to save ourselves from the inevitable and ultimately terminal conflicts of a world system based on competition rather than cooperation, an escape from the looming disasters of climate change, resource depletion, overpopulation, injustice, war, poverty and runaway military expenditures. Hugh Steadman, President, Sapiens, NZ

It's about time someone did this. All great visionary ideas seem mad or utopian—until they become reality. A global referendum on whether we, the people of the world, wish to democratically govern ourselves is about as sane a political idea as I can imagine. Syd Baumel, Winnipeg, Manitoba, National Council member, World Federalists Movement—Canada

---

Man is not imprisoned by habit. Great changes in him can be wrought by crisis - once that crisis can be recognized and understood. Norman Cousins

---

Nothing will end war unless the people refuse to go to war. Albert Einstein

Chapter 12

A constitutional framing conference

> **The people made the Constitution, and the people can unmake it. It is the creature of their own will, and lives only by their will.** John Marshall
> (He meant the U.S. *Constitution*, but the principle stands.)

Any democratic government, at any level, world, national, provincial (or state) or municipal, must be a "government of laws," and the primary or foundational law is, of course, a constitution (or a charter). Vote World Government has a curious dilemma, in that we expect we'll be able to successfully authorize the creation of a democratic world government, but that institution can't work unless we also create a document that spells out the *principles* involved, *the ways things are supposed to work*, its powers, and areas of authority or responsibility.[193] The DWG, once it exists, can adopt laws to give effect to these principles, and of course a world supreme court would be responsible for interpreting the constitution, and laws promulgated by the DWG. However, we must face the fact that in the earliest stages of this involved process, we are probably *not* going to have both the proverbial cart and the proverbial horse at the right place at exactly the same time.[194]

> **The enumeration in the [U.S.] Constitution of certain rights shall not be construed to deny or disparage others retained by the people.** Ninth Amendment, United States *Constitution*

To continue the metaphor, we will need more than one horse and one cart. Without a mandate from a successful global referendum, we can't even create a democratic world government. (We can create an *un*democratic world government without all the bother of consulting the people, but that is not what is best for humanity or the planet.) And without a realistic plan to create a DWG, there is no point in trying to write a world constitution,

---

[193] It will not be Vote World Government alone that brings this all together and writes the draft constitution. It will take a broad coalition of NGOs, governments and other parties to do this part of the process, and do it well.

[194] See Appendix #5 for a chart of hoped-for or anticipated developments. Note the timing and the overlap of these various developments.

because without it, all of the various actions of the DWG would lack formal authority.

As all democrats know, democracy is usually a messy business, and the creation of a DWG promises to be quite messy. There are people who believe that *before anything else* should happen, we must first draft a world constitution. But history is not likely to unfold according to that plan. Some non-governmental organizations have been working on a constitution for the world for many decades,[195] and the fact that very few people are even aware of this Herculean effort is evidence that the "purist" approach is not likely to succeed. And if we had an elected democratic world government and no constitution, that may be the equivalent of having a horse and a cart, but no road to travel on.

> **Non-violence is the greatest force at the disposal of mankind. It is mightier than the mightiest weapon of destruction devised by the ingenuity of man.** Mahatma Gandhi

The necessary spadework can proceed while evidence of public support is still being gathered by the global referendum that is now underway. A successful and completed referendum will change the equation ... the people will have authorized the creation of a DWG. The rather obvious next step would be to ask the people to ratify (or not) a proposed world constitution in a second world referendum, ideally in conjunction with the election of the first DWG representatives (if only because of the size of the logistical problems associated with conducting any global vote). Such a doubled-up procedure would also lay to rest the critics who would surely argue after the fact that without a draft constitution waiting in the wings, the people had no detailed idea what they were voting for in the referendum.

While perhaps unusual, there is no compelling reason why preparations for these two steps (the planning of a global general election by an electoral commission and the drafting of the world constitution by other means) can not proceed alongside the gathering of the mandate from the first global referendum, and because of the urgency of our situation, there is reason to begin those preparations as soon as possible. Two things have thwarted all earlier attempts to establish a world government—a serious global crisis,

---

[195] One is the World Constitution and Parliament Association. There exist many models for "world federations," but they involve leaving national governments at the top of the power heap, whereas our proposal concerns not a federation of nations, but a directly-elected world parliament, within which elected politicians represent the people living in their respective constituencies, not the nation from which they come or in which they live. For more, see Appendix #3.

and a means of authorizing the institution needed to implement all the provisions of a world constitution. Now we have the former, in spades, and we have the latter in the global referendum strategy.

We will need a draft constitution to "put to the people" at the same time as DWG constituencies will need to be established. If it is possible to get this process done in a decade, as we dare to hope, that means that in 2018 or earlier, there will be a worldwide voting exercise, where people will vote for a representative to the DWG and, at the same time, they will be able to vote "yes" or "no" to the draft world constitution. And here is an extremely important insight. *If the draft constitution fails to be ratified, the election of representatives would still be valid.* However, we won't have to reconstitute the World Electoral Commission, because by then we would have authorized a new group of players (MGPs) to "act on our behalf," and it would be up to them to decide how to move the constitutional process forward from there.

At the end of WWII our then (national) representatives formed the UN simply by signing a charter that they had drafted. The same process could apply here, though there would be more signatories. At least in this case the people will have had a direct voice in naming their representatives, and the people will have been given advance knowledge of the proposed organization (700+ directly-elected political representatives authorized and empowered to deal with supranational matters). This is not the same as the ratification that would emerge from a second global referendum, but it would carry more legitimacy than 100+ signatories appointed by national governments, many of whom were not democracies, in the 1940s. Although this way of moving ahead is not perfect, there is nothing stopping us from proceeding this way *until* a redrafted constitution can be developed and put to the people at a later date (meaning if the referendum on the first draft did not get the required 67% support).

Today's [U.S.] Constitution is a realistic document of freedom only because of several corrective amendments. Those amendments speak to a sense of decency and fairness that I and other Blacks cherish.
Thurgood Marshall (1908 - 1993), top aide to Bill Clinton and the first African-American Supreme Court Justice, in his book, *We The People*

If we had a powerful global mandate in hand right now for the creation of the DWG, the question would inevitably arise: "Where is the foundation document?" Every country has a constitution (or charter), as do all service clubs, unions, citizens' associations, even companies (in their articles of incorporation). Constitutions are, in a word, "indispensable," if only to be certain that a mission statement is available to explain why the organization exists and what it is expected to accomplish (its "mandate"). Of course a constitution (charter) also has to include a structure, and an explanation of how power is exercised, and how the decision-makers are elected. And of course it must include an amending formula so it can be revised or updated at a later date, as experience and future events dictate.

As mentioned earlier, if national governments were allowed to write the constitution for the DWG, we would end up with another United Nations, which is *not* what is needed. To refuse the offer of *helpful* participation from national governments (in the framing of a world constitution or the funding of the process by which a constitution is drafted) would be folly, but to let national governments run the show or even wield a veto over the content of a world constitution would be a much greater folly. A democratic world government should exist *not* to represent the 194 nations of the world, but to represent the human race as a whole (although every elected MGP is also there to represent all the citizens who live in his or her DWG constituency). National governments can help us generate a draft world constitution, but they must not bully other participants in the drafting process in the way they traditionally bully each other. Keeping national governments at arm's length is necessary because of their failure at the two pivotal moments in history when the League of Nations and the UN were designed. *Humanity cannot afford to make the same mistakes a third time.*

> **The Constitution is not an instrument for the government to restrain the people, it is an instrument for the people to restrain the government ... lest it come to dominate our lives and interests.** Patrick Henry, American lawyer, patriot and orator

The DWG must exist to serve the needs of the human race and to represent its interests ... *not* to please national governments. In a decade or so, I hope to be represented *directly* at four levels; at the municipal level, at the provincial (or state, in the USA) level, at the national level, and at the world level. I cannot promise that there won't be disagreements, especially between national governments and the DWG, but once it is clear that *all* the weapons of omnicide have been dismantled (that may take a century), and once the natural environment has been rescued and protected to allow for the permanent survival of life on Earth (and that may take *more* than a century), I expect these disputes among the various levels of government will diminish in number and intensity. (In Canada, and in virtually all other democracies, although there are many disputes between the provinces and the national government, no party even considers war as a possible means of resolving those disputes.)

> **Warmaking doesn't stop warmaking. If it did, our problems would have stopped millennia ago.** Colman McCarthy, former journalist and now peace educator

The *political impetus* to write such a world constitution and the perceived need for writing it will likely evolve from the emerging global mandate, as manifested through the referendum. We cannot know the future for sure, but we should expect the two processes—the actual execution of the global referendum and the preparation of a basic constitution for the world—to overlap (see Appendix #5). *If* the online vote count rises into the millions, and tens of millions, and then hundreds of millions, and *if* the referendum is passing strongly (at least 67% "yes" votes), people will realize that we really are making this profound change of direction as a united species, and the pressure will increase to get a draft constitution done.

> **We have grasped the mystery of the atom and rejected the Sermon on the Mount ... The world has achieved brilliance without conscience. Ours is a world of nuclear giants and ethical infants. We know more about war than we know about peace, more about killing than we know about living.** U.S. Army General Omar N. Bradley

If the global mandate is one-third complete, let us say, and few people expect the other two-thirds of the vote to yield any different result from the strong "yes" result of the first third, then we can all see a day coming when it *will* be finished, and those would be the conditions that would *compel* the calling of a global[196] conference for the drafting of a world constitution (if the drafting process is not already underway, as I hope it would be by then). As the global mandate grows, a global conference simply has to be called, and in time it will produce a draft constitution to present to the people for ratification.

---

[196] Please do not substitute the word "international" for the word "global." They do have similar meanings, but we do not need to refer to nations in our effort to be the founders of a global government any more than we need to refer to cities, provinces or galaxies. "Global" says it, and says it best. Also, there may be work done on a draft constitution before this global conference is called, and I hope we will be able to persuade the Canadian government to call a meeting of NGOs, constitutional lawyers and others to prepare for such a global "framing" conference.

The collection of the global mandate required to authorize the creation of the DWG may take five years or so,[197] and then it may be another five years before we elect the first crop of MGPs, so let us tentatively assess that there is a ten-year "window" in which to draft a world constitution that will satisfy a significant majority of people from all parts of the world. If work starts on a draft in 2009, that should give us a result by 2013, at a time when the World Electoral Commission should be well into its work of preparing for the first global general election.

> **The Constitution does not grant rights, it recognizes them.** Jason Laumark (He meant the U.S. *Constitution*, but the principle stands.)

As mentioned earlier, we want a draft constitution to be ready to put to the people of the world at the same time as the first global general election, so people can vote for or against the constitution at the same time as they vote for a political candidate to be their DWG representative. We do need to be prepared for the possibility that the adoption of this constitution may be just the beginning of a permanent struggle by parties of all descriptions (and aspirations) to accomplish a particular global goal, the difference being that now, these struggles *can't* be carried on by force of arms and *must* yield to the interests of the human race as a whole, as expressed through the new DWG.

Because national governments, to a significant extent, *are* the problem, they simply *cannot* be allowed to control the process by which the world constitution is drafted. On the other hand, drafters must recognize that it is unlikely that national governments would allow us[198] to create a DWG that does not provide for their security and freedom (again, with the exceptions of their *former* freedom to make wars or trash the environment). In return for this unavoidable commitment by the DWG,[199] we expect that national governments will in turn provide the funding, technical guidance and other kinds of assistance that may be required to complete this mutually beneficial project.

It should be possible to have a final draft constitution ready to submit to voters worldwide at the same time as the election of the first MGPs is

---

[197] It can be done much sooner if individuals and NGOs get on their horses and ride like the wind … or it could take longer … or it could never happen, if an effort by powerful interests stops us.

[198] Remember, at this time, they are still able to use force to get what they want.

[199] This is a commitment that should be undertaken by the DWG even without any need or request for reassurance by national governments. Nations per se are not the problem; it is the multiplicity of so-called *sovereign* nations that is the problem, as explained earlier.

held. While too much haste can lead to foolish errors and bad judgements, every effort should be made to press forward as quickly as possible.

In the same way that juries are sometimes sequestered to reach a verdict, it might be a useful idea to hire a few acknowledged experts from academia, some respected NGO people, plus some "inperts" from various vocations (retired judges, former diplomats, former heads of governments, eminent scholars, etc.), lock them in a hotel (with translators and every service they may possibly require), and tell them not to emerge until they have a rough draft on which a larger group of conferees can build. As they prepare such a skeletal document for circulation, the organizers of this framing conference should keep in mind the efforts of NGOs that have been working for years to construct a constitution for the world.

The above could be one of the steps taken as part of the suggestion that Canada sponsor this preliminary constitutional framing conference. It has also been suggested that the Canadian government is in a position to fund this conference. This effort can start any time the finances are there; it does not have to wait until the vote count in the global referendum is eye-popping impressive.

Work may soon be under way to prepare a proposal along these lines for the Canadian government. The Canadian government will not just hand over the required $50 million and wish us luck, but as the vote count in the global referendum swells, and as the media comes to understand that this campaign is for real, and may well succeed, pressure will surely rise for the Canadian government to do what it can to facilitate matters. Canada is a wealthy nation, and it can afford this, even if the cost of such a conference is $150 million. Still, Canada is often subjected to immense pressures from our American neighbours, so we hope the global referendum campaign in the USA takes off strongly ... and that the American debate can begin as to how the world's only remaining national superpower should prepare for the day when there is a new democratic world government in place, supported by the entire human race.

> The [U.S.] *Constitution* ... divides power ... among branches of government precisely so that we may resist the temptation to concentrate power in one location as an expedient solution to the crisis of the day. Unknown. Source: U.S. Supreme Court, 1992, New York v. United States, 505 U.S., 144

The plan for Canada to start this off is not an essential part of the overall strategy, but it sure would help. While this preliminary constitutional drafting conference would be hosted and paid for by the government of

Canada, it is important to accept that it will not be conducted or controlled by the government of Canada. Rather, it must be a shared undertaking by two equal partners (government and civil society) with a common goal, but with access to Canadian government resources. (Of course a plain language final document would be best, since "legalese" just confuses people.)

Time will tell if this plan will work, but at first blush it appears hopeful, sensible and affordable. The idea for a preliminary round of deliberations by a group of people having widely representative but perhaps strongly divergent perspectives is to build on and learn from the so-called Ottawa Process, which is a process by which the 1997 *Mine Ban Treaty*[200] was written and established as new international law literally at lightning speed—in spite of *strong* opposition from the American government and others. [201]

By taking this approach, we hope to avoid the trap whereby national governments decide the agenda and make all the critical decisions. This is exactly how the League of Nations and the UN managed to *not* be up to the job of preventing war and governing the world. We hope it will be possible to produce an acceptable draft constitution that people would see as fair and representative of their dreams, aspirations and needs. Notwithstanding the limited nature of the process, we hope people will remember our need for prudent haste, and conclude that this document represents a reasonable and proper birthing for a democratic institution.

> **Everything that is really great and inspiring is created by the individual who can labor in freedom.** Albert Einstein

One final word about this. Drafting a constitution isn't nuclear physics, and it also isn't brain surgery. It's been done hundreds of times for nations, often centuries ago, with quite good results in many cases. While obviously prepared for small constituencies with more limited ranges of needs, many of them were signed, sealed and delivered within months, rather than years. I mention this because there will be those who will pull at their hair and wail to the moon about how this simply cannot be done. The bottom line is it *can* be done, if only because it *has* to be done. Beware of those who claim to *know* it can't be done. They are not in any position to predict the future, and if we are not careful, they will obstruct our efforts to do what it takes to secure a peaceful future for the world and for our species. As the Robert

---

[200] Often called the *Landmines Treaty* or the Ottawa Convention, its official title is the *Convention on the Prohibition of the Use, Stockpiling, Production and Transfer of Anti-Personnel Mines and on Their Destruction*, or, for short, the *Mine Ban Treaty*.
[201] See Chapter 14 for a full explanation of how this was done.

Hutchins' group said back in 1948 (see Appendix #6), "World government is necessary, therefore it is possible."

The liberties of none are safe unless the liberties of all are protected.
U.S. Supreme Court Justice William O. Douglas

The world needs to be governed by constitutional law, not by war. True law acts directly on the individual, not on sovereign states or whole communities as such. Genuine law is law that can be enforced on individual law-breakers (not on Sovereign States, which is impossible without the use of military force). Preferably it derives from a democratic legislature, applies equally to every separate member of the community, and is peaceably enforceable through the courts. Harold S. Bidmead, *Tilting at Windbags: The Autobiography of a World Federalist*

Humankind continues to face the threat of nuclear annihilation. Today's hesitation leads to tomorrow's destruction. The fates of all of us are bound together here on earth. There can be no survival for any without peaceful coexistence for all. Takeshi Araki, Mayor of Hiroshima, 6 August 1985

Since I do not foresee that atomic energy is to be a great boon for a long time, I have to say that for the present it is a menace. Perhaps it is well that it should be. It may intimidate the human race into bringing order into its international affairs, which, without the presence of fear, it would not do. Albert Einstein

---

People are never more insecure than when they become obsessed with their fears at the expense of their dreams. Norman Cousins

---

There is nothing easier than lopping off heads and nothing harder than developing ideas. Fyodor Dostoevsky

Chapter 13

Fast tracking the global referendum on DWG

Be the change you want to see in the world. Mahatma Gandhi, major political and spiritual leader of the Indian Independence Movement, the pioneer of resistance through mass civil disobedience

I dithered for weeks about whether to include this chapter. I worried that people might think I was being unrealistic if I said there was a way to collect the global mandate in less than a year. Then I realized that it should not matter a hoot what people think of me personally, so, since a "warp-speed" strategy *does* exist, and *could theoretically* work, I offer this concept.

H.L. Menken—journalist, beer drinker and sage—said that for every complex problem there is a solution that is simple, neat and wrong. Michael Robotham, in his novel, *Suspect*

It is impossible to accurately predict the future, but it is not impossible to make what risk-takers may call an "educated guess." My educated guess is that ten years may well be too long a time for this referendum process. WWIII may break out before we're done, or we may reach the "point of no return" on climate change. So I "put on my thinking cap" (as teachers used to say back in the 1950s), and I asked myself this critical question: If we had *no choice* but to collect the global mandate in less than a year, how would we go about trying to do that? Maybe there is a way that is "simple, neat" and yet *not* "wrong."

Never doubt that a small group of thoughtful, committed citizens can change the world; indeed it is the only thing that ever has. Margaret Mead, American cultural anthropologist

One can think of many ideas that could contribute to such a "fast track" plan. I listed a fair number of those in Chapter 4—printing the global referendum ballot in newspapers, having schools, offices or churches hand out the printed ballot to their people, arranging for a municipal referendum in your home town, letting other people who don't have the Internet use your computer to cast a vote online on our website, collecting paper ballots and doing the imputing on our website, and, of course, getting our draft UN resolution passed in the General Assembly (see Appendix #2 for the UN resolution).

> **We are struggling badly in the world, and have not adopted a proper solution to our problems…. We need to either create new organizations or reform the United Nations. We need a global parliament … and a global ministry of defense…. We will not allow anyone to violate the rules or else the global forces will bring order. This is what is still needed.** Lech Walesa, former Polish President, 2004

But is it possible, in this new digital age, that one person could light an informational match that triggers a bonfire of truly global proportions (not literally of course, but figuratively)? Is it possible that one person with some brains, guts and two hours of free time can do something so incisive that it creates a "multiplier effect" that ends up as a completed, collected global mandate for democratic world government (DWG) in less than one year? In a word, yes.

> **A journey of a thousand miles must begin with a single step.** Lao Tzu, ancient Chinese philosopher

Chain letters, pyramid schemes and some of the common multi-level marketing schemes are immoral and illegal because they depend on a false hope of easy riches—they are actually *designed* to steal money from people. But they work *up to a point* and, sadly, people do fall for them. However, if we were to modify a pyramid scheme so that *no money at all* was involved, and the only prize at the end was the achievement of world peace through world law, surely no one can object, and (one would hope) some people might even break out in spontaneous applause. So, let's launch a pyramid scheme like that, a *good* one, a "chain" type of event that can end up playing a crucial role in eliminating war and saving the Earth. Here is your "fast-track assignment."

Go to www.voteworldgovernment.org and vote "yes" (we are not neutral in this; we are *for* the DWG), and then, **within one week** of casting your own "yes" vote, get **two more** people to vote "yes" in the global referendum. Of course anyone can vote "no" if they want, and anyone can go to the website and vote "yes" or "no" without your encouragement, but if they want to be part of the fast track, do **not** let your two "recruits" vote **as part of your chain** unless they are **willing to promise** that in addition to casting their own "yes" votes, they will also get **two more people** (that's two more **each**) to vote "yes" in your chain, and make the **same promise** about **the week following** their own vote. On the next page, I have put a graphic presentation, so you can imagine this process better.

At the bottom of all the tributes paid to democracy is the little man [or woman], **walking into the little booth, with a little pencil, making a little cross on a little bit of paper.** Winston Churchill

---

Power tends to corrupt and absolute power corrupts absolutely. Lord Acton (John Emerich Edward Dalberg-Acton), English historian, 1887

... the emergency committee of atomic scientists, having explored for two years all means other than world government for making responsible the control of atomic energy effective [meaning nuclear weapons, really, and by implication, all weapons of mass destruction], **has become convinced that no other method than world government can be expected to prove effective, and that the attainment of world government is therefore the most urgent problem now facing mankind.** United Nations Resolution (1948)

Either war is obsolete or men are. Buckminster Fuller, American architect, visionary, inventor, *New Yorker*, January 8, 1966

A human being fashions his consequences as surely as he fashions his goods or his dwelling. Nothing that he says, thinks or does is without consequences. Norman Cousins

---

Terrorism is the war of the poor, and war is the terrorism of the rich.
Sir Peter Ustinov

Can we collect a global mandate for democratic world government in less than one year?

Sure we can, if the first "yes" voter brings in 2 _more_ "yes" voters in 1 week, and receives promises that those 2 will each do the same thing and bring in 2 other _new_ "yes" voters the following week, etc. (See below.)

GRAPHIC PRESENTATION

Time (after 1st vote is cast)	New "yes" votes during this period	**Total "yes"** votes so far
Week #1	2	(first 1 + new 2 =) **3**
Week #2	4	(old 3 + new 4 =) **7**
Week #3	8	(old 7 + new 8 =) **15**
Week #4	16	**31**
Week #5	32	**63**
Week #6	64	**127**
Week #7	128	**255**
Week #8	256	**511**
Week #9	512	**1,000** (approx.)
Week #10	1,000 (approx.)	**2,000**
Week #11	2,000	**4,000**
Week #12	4,000	**8,000**
Week #13	8,000	**16,000**
Week #14	16,000	**32,000**
Week #15	32,000	**64,000**
Week #16	64,000	**128,000**
Week #17	128,000	**256,000**
Week #18	256,000	**512,000**
Week #19	512,000	**1 million** (approx.)
Week #20	1 million (approx.)	**2 million**
Week #21	2 million	**4 million**
Week #22	4 million	**8 million**
Week #23	8 million	**16 million**
Week #24	16 million	**32 million**
Week #25	32 million	**64 million**
Week #26	64 million	**128 million**
Week #27	128 million	**256 million**
Week #28	256 million	**512 million**
Week #29	512 million	**1 billion** (approx.)
Week #30	1 billion (approx.)	**2 billion** _Enough to win!_
Week #31	2 billion	**3+ billion** _A landslide victory!_

This is admittedly an improbable scenario, but _it could work_!

Chain voting checklist

1   Did I cast my own "yes" vote at www.voteworldgovernment.org?   ____

2   Did I tell my "recruiter" I voted, and that I promise to start two chains?   ____

3   Did I get one other person to vote and promise to continue the chain?   ____

4   Did I get a second person to vote and promise to continue the chain?   ____

5   Did my first recruit *confirm* that he or she got two more new recruits?   ____

6   Did my second recruit *confirm* that he or she got two more recruits?   ____

7   Did I report that my two recruits voted *and got their two recruits each?*   ____

8   Did I start a new chain if one of my recruits failed to do his or her job?   ____

9   Did I report that my #1 through #6 (see below) have all done their jobs?   ____

10   Did I consider starting new chains even if I've already done my bit?   ____

Below, fill in the names of the *direct* recruits in your two chains (#1 and #2), then fill in the names (#3, #4, #5 and #6) of the next "generation" of yes voters on your two chains. You must confirm that your two direct recruits (#1 and #2) did their job *in full*, but it may be a good idea to confirm that their four new recruits also did *their* job IN FULL, and did it within one week of casting their own votes. Each of these new people should of course fill in their own name beside the word "Me" (on the left, below) and carry on from there.

Please print or write <u>clearly</u>

```
                                          ( #3_____
                                          (
                    ( #1_____    ( #4_____
                    (                      (
  Me  _____   (
                    (                      ( #5_____
                    ( #2_____    (
                                          ( #6_____
```

There is nothing stopping anyone from starting more than two chains, of course, and the sooner we get to our goal of 2 billion or so votes the sooner we will have the democratic world government. <u>If possible, do not write on this page.</u> Instead, make a photocopy and **print** on it. If you have 10 checkmarks and seven names written in, you are encouraged to scan your filled-in photocopy of this page and send a copy to us (as a .jpg attachment to an email) for all future generations to see. Our address is voteworldgovernment@webruler.com. (Please, do not expect us to respond—we are far too busy to answer everyone, but you can rely on us to keep all these records, *permanently.*)

Chapter 14

Civil society and the "Ottawa Process"

We must apply at the global level that which we apply at the national level: democracy. Dominique de Villepin, Radio France Interview May 22, 2003 [Originally in French: Il faut appliquer au niveau mondial ce que nous appliquons au niveau national: la démocratie.]

Having discussed what the individual can do in Chapter 13 (and elsewhere), let us look at what organizations can do if they choose to help out.

In the words of Mary-Wynne Ashford, we are "… at the beginning of a global social revolution. This revolution is the rise of civil society bringing conscience to guide the behaviour of governments and financial institutions."[202] This chapter examines "civil society" and the role it played in the so-called Ottawa Process, with a view to identifying the important elements of that process, the lessons to be learned from it, and its possible application to this project. If we can link the global reach of the Internet with the power of nation states and the moral force of civil society, as was done in the Ottawa Process (to ban landmines), we may be able to watch the inaugural session of the world parliament quite soon indeed.

What is civil society?

For a brief backgrounder, here again is Mary-Wynne Ashford:

> The growth of civil society is a response to the failure of governments, both capitalist and communist, to address the concerns of humanity. Now that the communist model has been discredited, we can see more clearly democracy's vulnerability to corruption, as well as the shortcomings of the free market economy. The new superpower is more than just public opinion; it is public engagement in decision-making. [See James F. Moore's book in the bibliography.]
>
> This idea of two superpowers captures the essence of our current situation; one power is based on military domination and control of people by force; the other power is based on cooperation

---

[202] *Enough Blood Shed*, Mary-Wynne Ashford (M.D., PhD) with Guy Dauncey, New Society Publishers pages 2-3. Ashford was a co-president of International Physicians for the Prevention of Nuclear War. She currently heads an initiative of Physicians for Global Survival, "Responsibility to Care: The Physicians' Call to End War."

and the rule of law. The future is far from clear. The second superpower will flourish only if the huge number of people who want an end to violence, terror and war continue to demand to be heard....

All three pillars of society – government, economy and culture – are essential and must interact to benefit society, but one sector must not take over the role of another. Throughout history, people – alone and in groups – have constrained the attempts by rulers and the wealthy to assume unbridled power. Today there is an imbalance because governments and huge multinational corporations have become enmeshed. *The result is that fundamental needs of society are not being met – especially the need to ensure a sustainable environment. Furthermore, the disproportionate influence of militarization is distorting democracy.* (Emphasis added.)

The meaning of "civil society" is still evolving. The Centre for Civil Society's initial working definition is not to be interpreted as a rigid statement, but it reads in part as follows:

Civil societies are often populated by organisations such as registered charities, development non-governmental organisations, community groups, women's organisations, faith-based organisations, professional associations, trades unions, self-help groups, social movements, business associations, coalitions and advocacy groups.

The Centre for Civil Society's website[203] goes on to say

The EU [European Union], like other international institutions, has a long way to go in trying to accommodate the frequently divergent interests of non-governmental organisations and citizen groups. There is increasing recognition that international and national governments have to open up to civil society institutions.

For the purposes of this book, let us say "civil society" simply means "us"—"we, the people"—and the organizations (other than government) through which we are involved in the affairs of our local, regional, national or global communities.

International law slowly evolved over centuries of conflict to fill vacuums felt by warring nations in their search for "civilized" relations with their neighbours ... and new ways of acquiring more than their fair share of Earth's riches. It has gained momentum in the last hundred years, and broadened its scope from establishing norms of behaviour between or among nations to recognizing and proclaiming the rights of individuals that

---

[203] http://www.lse.ac.uk/collections/CCS/Default.htm, Centre for Civil Society, London School of Economics

must be recognized by states. Unfortunately, as a result of short-sighted, perceived self-interests, the nation states failed to give international law the power that it needs to enforce the fine words they imbued it with.

In the past, governments and rulers often entered into treaties or agreements with little or no intention of abiding by them. These attitudes are gradually changing. The UN *Charter* and various UN declarations have become the recognized standards for civilized behaviour, and governments of all stripes are embarrassed if they are seen to fail to meet those standards. Civil society is learning how to pressure governments to meet the standards established by the international community. In recent decades, however, it seems that nation states are choosing to side with corporations, and are placing economics at the top of their agenda. Many have turned something of a deaf ear to their people, and used military solutions to suppress dissent. As a result, it is now widely recognized in civil society that we need a new platform for our voices, to address our priorities and concerns, to meet our needs and, ultimately, to save our world. In short, we need a democratic world government.

> **We believe that we can protect ourselves against inter-national wars only through the establishment of constitutional life in world affairs, and that such universal Law must be created in conformity with the democratic process, by freely elected and responsible representatives.**
> Angela Harkavy, *The Earth Charter*

Civil society, though often unrecognized, has always played an important part within nations or societies. It is, however, a relative newcomer to the world stage. Civil society draws its strength from "common" people coming together to fill at least some of the voids resulting from the neglect or inability of the nation state to fulfill the needs of its own people. Although it is gathering strength, civil society is still a minor player on the global level, due in part to an array of structural difficulties that limit the ability of its member-organisations to exert significant influence on transnational forms of state power.

Social movements tend to rely on cultural impact. Their success often depends on their position, being outside formal state structures. But therein lies their weakness, particularly when satisfaction of their demands must come *from* a state. Social movements usually experience cycles of support, and their leaders have difficulty matching their peaks of mobilization to the small windows of opportunity that present themselves from time to time when the state is most vulnerable to their influence.

These problems are greatly magnified when a movement must move beyond its nationally based boundaries to influence other states involved in activities that the movement is trying to change. In such situations, the movement must forge links with like-minded movements in those other states and develop mutually supporting strategies. This may partly explain why interstate relations have been relatively devoid of popular or electoral influence. And like governments, some civil society organisations are hampered by hidden agendas, leadership egos and lack of money.

These then are the challenges. I believe the time is right and the need so great that we, the caring and engaged members of civil society, can and must overcome the above obstacles and assure our survival and our well-being through new means, new institutions.

The Ottawa Process: a sketch

When the 1996 review of the *Convention on Certain Conventional Weapons* failed to result in significant progress, a political initiative was launched in October of that year. A group of 40 supportive states joined a core group of NGOs determined to eliminate the scourge of landmines. This initiative resulted in 123 states signing the *Mine Ban Treaty* in Ottawa, Canada in December, 1997.

This astonishingly successful initiative is sometimes referred to as the "Ottawa Process." It grew out of the frustration felt by a few "middle power" nations (such as Canada) and a small number of NGOs over the failure of the global state community to address the deplorable suffering inflicted daily on innocent people, long after a military conflict ends. Although all parties deserve credit, I think it is not unfair to suggest that the advocacy and the mobilization efforts of the 1000+ involved NGOs turned the tide in favour of the treaty.

The process was interesting and innovative. After the failed review conference, Canada hosted a subsequent conference, whose primary objectives were to develop a declaration states would sign to signal their intention to ban antipersonnel mines, and an *Agenda for Action*, outlining concrete steps meant to reach such a ban. The concluding comments by Lloyd Axworthy, then foreign minister of Canada, were the catalyst needed to break through the barriers that had for so very long barred the way to a solution. The Canadian government, through Mr. Axworthy, challenged the world to return to Canada in one year to sign an international treaty banning antipersonnel landmines. After that, a small and determined staff organized the efforts of thousands of dedicated volunteers and the Ottawa process gained unstoppable momentum.[204]

A treaty was drafted by Austria and developed in a series of meetings in Vienna, Bonn, Brussels and Oslo over the course of 1997 while the like-minded governments formed a "Core Group" that, in close cooperation with over 1,000 NGOs and international organizations, helped steer the Ottawa Process. Significantly, the "friends of the Ottawa treaty" spanned the regions of the world and included representatives in both mine-affected countries and mine-producing countries. When it appeared this initiative was going to succeed, great pressure was brought to bear on the participating national governments by opponents of the ban. However, thanks to public support mobilized by the NGOs in their home countries, these states withstood the pressure to weaken the terms of the treaty.

But the job of civil society did not end with the signing of the treaty. The coalition needed to ensure that at least 40 states ratified the treaty they had signed in order to bring it into force. Work still continues in an effort a) to have all states sign and ratify the treaty, b) to ensure the signatory nations live up to their obligations under the treaty and, c) to retain the active support of civil society in the de-mining, rehabilitation and casualty support efforts that would have to continue for decades in order to repair the terrible damage to the environment and mitigate the human suffering caused by these indiscriminate weapons.

Important elements of the process included a unique, open and inclusive partnership of equals (civil society and governments) and the sharing of a common objective, unconstrained by traditional diplomatic protocol. Small and middle powers played the leading roles in a process that unfolded with unprecedented speed, proving that rapid progress *can* be made in international affairs. It clearly confirmed that: a) complex issues require a multifaceted approach, b) a partnership can pay great dividends, and c) formal deadlines for action are useful and the demonstration of broad public support is important.

You cannot control war; you can only abolish it. Those who shrug this off as idealistic are the real enemies of peace – the real war mongers. *Revitalizing a Nation, quotes of General Douglas MacArthur*, correlation and captions by John M. Pratt, Heritage Foundation, Inc., 1952, page 89

---

[204] Coalitions of national organisations formed in many countries. International organisations such as the Red Cross participated. Diana, Princess of Wales aided to the raising of public awareness enormously and the group's ability to fund a real media campaign greatly assisted in developing public support.

So, how can we adapt the lessons of the Ottawa Process to this significantly larger and more complex undertaking? It could prove to be relatively simple, although that is not to say it will be easy. With the support of a goodly number of like-minded states, there already exist recognized and respected UN entities which could be enlisted to provide the expert elements that civil society requires to build the foundations for a democratic world government.[205]

The Ottawa Process demonstrated that solutions to problems that the nations have wrestled with for decades can be found and implemented in a few years. It showed the value of partnerships in an open, inclusive process that incorporates coordinated dialogue among professionals and in meetings between states. In the process under examination, it is suggested that civil society representatives also have seats at a table of equals when a meeting of supportive states takes place.

One possible adaptation of the Ottawa Process

All of the activities needed to establish a DWG, set out in the brief outline below, can and should be carried out simultaneously. They are mutually supportive.

First, we need to establish and provide evidence that there is a mandate of the people to create a democratic world government. Vote World Government (the NGO behind the global referendum proposal) has already begun to disseminate information and gather evidence that such a mandate exists. If civil society supporters (and other individuals) do their part as suggested in Chapter 13, the built-in multiplier effect should get the overall job done in a few years. Of course early *state* supporters, as members of the UN, are in a position to greatly facilitate the process in their home nation (they could conduct a national referendum on the DWG issue) and through the UN (they could co-sponsor the UN resolution shown in Appendix #2). But we cannot wait around to see how that situation might turn out.

Second, we need to assemble a core group of widely respected NGOs to guide the worldwide mobilization process and elicit the support of their national states to this endeavour. They would be responsible for encouraging the multiplier effect among the various organizations which make up the civil society of their regions (in addition to mobilizing their own base of supporters to vote, online or otherwise, they could also commit to bringing two more NGOs into the process). Together they would work in partnership to build the support needed among the people of their various cultures and constituencies, building a growing list of

---

[205] Remember the workers' slogan of WWII: "Give us the tools and we will finish the job."

"Friends of Democratic World Government." These "Friends" in turn would provide more of the pressure needed to ensure that their governments become supporters. A world famous and well-respected celebrity "patron" wouldn't hurt, or a musical star in search of a new song, for that matter. Add a few wealthy foundations and philanthropists and we *will* get the job done.

Third, a core group of civil society organizations (CSOs), non-governmental organizations (NGOs) and supportive states will work together to ensure the development of a draft constitution establishing the democratic world government. This draft needs to be approved by the human race, the "global community," and it should be available within a few years so that it can be voted on by the people alongside the first general election of representatives to the world parliament. There are many existing precedents from which the drafters can select the best provisions, so we need not concern ourselves too greatly here with the details of this part of the process. There are many highly respected independent resource institutions as well as government departments that can and should be enlisted to the process—universities, national law associations, the World Court and the International Law Commission of the UN, to name but a few. Also, the groups overseeing the drafting of the constitution will no doubt each have their own independent expert advisors.

The constitution drafting process must be completely open, and a shared responsibility of equals. Its development must be free of hidden agendas, political interference and undue influence by any of the stakeholders. The drafters will no doubt be fully conscious of the fact that in the end, the inhabitants of the global village will have the final say, and that this may be our last opportunity to get it right. But—and this is important—the drafters must recognize and accommodate, at least in the beginning, the fact that the real world is dominated by nation states and multinational corporations. (I don't think anyone can predict what these accommodations will be until we are actually faced with the inevitable pressures that will be brought to bear on the core group.)

Fourth, DWG electoral boundaries will need to be determined. A general approach to how this might be accomplished is set out in Chapter 8 and Appendix #3, so I will not deal with this part of the process in detail here. Presumably, when the initiative has gathered sufficient momentum to get to that point, this aspect of the journey to democratic world governance will be relatively easy to wrap up. All people will want to be represented in the new world parliament and no nation state would have much to gain by refusing its people an opportunity to participate.

Fifth, the physical structures and support staffs needed by the fledgling DWG will be determined at the time by the DWG, and it is assumed that the necessary powers for their funding will be incorporated into the world constitution, and need not be discussed here.

> For I dipt into the future, far as human eye could see,
> Saw the Vision of the world, and all the wonders that could be;
> Till the war-drum throbb'd no longer and the battle flags were furl'd
> In the Parliament of man, the Federation of the world.
> There the common sense of most shall hold a fretful realm in awe,
> And the kindly earth shall slumber, lapt in universal law.
>
> Alfred, Lord Tennyson, "Locksley Hall" (1837)[206]

By now you might be wondering, "It all seems so simple. Why wasn't this done before?" Well, it isn't exactly simple, but I hope by now you are convinced it can be done … *if* you and I and our friends and relatives and their acquaintances are able and willing to take a few minutes to vote, and urge others to do likewise.

To NGO or CSO leaders I say this. Although the constitutional framing process will require huge resources that (likely) only states can provide, getting the global referendum to a point where it has "Big Mo" ("momentum") will take little of your time and virtually no money. Do the math. The mandate of your organization will be *far* easier to realize with a DWG in place than it is now. Please ask your organization to join in with the "Friends of Democratic World Government," and ask other NGOs or CSOs to do likewise.

> **The UN must evolve towards a world government.** [Originally in French: L'ONU doit aller vers un gouvernement mondial.] Jacques Delors

> **Peace cannot be kept by force; it can only be achieved through understanding.** Albert Einstein

> **A dream you dream alone is only a dream. A dream you dream together is reality.** John Lennon, a member of The Beatles

---

[206] United States President Harry Truman, who oversaw the founding of the UN after WWII, kept these lines in his wallet.

Chapter 15

Conclusion

> **To jaw-jaw is always better than to war-war.** Winston Churchill

Democratic government may be a messy business, but it is surely always preferable to war, or to a non-democratic government, or to an absence of political structure where there is an obvious need for governance, as is the case right now at the global level. It is difficult (if not impossible) to argue convincingly that things would get *worse* than they are now if we were to build a new political body at the global level. I am not particularly interested in which side might win a tiresome debate on that hypothetical matter, since the status quo leads us to catastrophe in the near future. I am interested, however, in seeing the global referendum on DWG conducted, and I am interested in seeing the creation of the DWG ... soon.

> **A great wind is blowing and that gives you either imagination or a headache.** Catherine the Great

The day of the armed-and-war-capable city-state ended many centuries ago. The day of the tribal warlord is over too, even though a few are still in business. Terrorism (whether it is non-state, state-sponsored or religious— these distinctions matter little or nothing to the victims) and war are next on the agenda for tossing into the dustbin of history. The struggle to outlaw war and rid ourselves of terror is not going to be won by any one nation, or even a group of nations. Violence-for-gain in all its forms has to be banned by the people, by the human race, by our species *as a whole*, and not by sending national armies into another nation to do regime change,[207] but rather through a variety of pressures and incentives from a new people's parliament, meaning a democratic world government.

In a few years, the era of the armed-and-war-capable nation state must end too, because that is a precondition for the survival of humanity, as Albert Einstein (and many others) have said. The creation of a directly-elected, representative and democratic world government is surely the only

---

[207] Which is illegal under international law no matter how you package it.

realistic foundation on which we can tackle all of the other supranational problems that bedevil us—racism, climate change, pollution, HIV/AIDS, overpopulation, poverty, and more. A global referendum appears to be the only democratic instrument through which the human race could insist upon and authorize the construction and permanent operation of such an institution.

> **A world under law is realistic and attainable.** Former UN Secretary-General U Thant

Those who want democratic global governance *must* remember that democracy rests upon and requires the consent of the people, the consent of the governed. That principle applies globally as well as nationally or locally. Before trying to create a world parliament, we must get the necessary consent in hand so we know we are not imposing something on the human race that it does not want. We can easily reduce the goal to a simple ballot question such as: "Do you support the creation of a directly-elected, representative and democratic world government?" The Internet allows us to at least kick-start a global referendum on whether we ought to create such a new world body. The job of finishing a global referendum may well require the passage of a UN resolution and some participation by national governments, but that level of cooperation is unlikely to emerge until we have a "people-power parade" marching down the main street in every city and town in the world—figuratively speaking, anyway—a "yes" campaign that appears to be winning in all nations. Opinion polls are not enough (as mentioned earlier), but if the numbers in such opinion polls are favourable to our cause, they can help us prove our point and acquire allies.

> **Throughout history it has been the inaction of those who could have acted, the indifference of those who should have known better, the silence of the voice of justice when it mattered most, that has made it possible for evil to triumph.** Haile Selassie, then Emperor of Ethiopia, to an opening a Special Session of the UN General Assembly in Addis Ababa, 1963

Humanity is ready for a change in direction, and we expect that a powerful species-wide mandate (66.7%+) exists for the creation of a democratic world government. Reason and experience suggest that in addition to having enormous political weight, our "consent" (as expressed in the global mandate) is destined to evolve into an "authorization," an unprecedented global *command* that will have to be accepted as *legally binding*, and/or the political equivalent. The global referendum is a realistic strategy, and all that remains to be seen is whether we have what it takes to rise to the challenge, to rescue ourselves, and to basically grow up, as a species … finally.

We have reached a time in human history where "sovereignty" must be exercised on behalf of our species *as a whole*. We, the people, must take charge of the last few steps along the difficult road from yesteryear's jungle to tomorrow's peaceful and secure civilization. We must literally "civilize ourselves," lest we lose the struggle and exterminate ourselves. The UN should be an important part of all this,[208] and can play a constructive role. But make no mistake; if humanity goes to the trouble of conducting the global referendum to demand and authorize the creation of a democratic world government and the vote passes strongly, that mandate *must* be honoured, that institution *must* be created, and the DWG *must* play the *pre-eminent* role in establishing and maintaining a genuine and permanent peace in the world. If we can at last rid the human condition of all terrorism and war, we would no more go back to those obscene traditions than we would go back to the practice of human sacrifice, or slavery, or any of the other hideous abominations from our sad and embarrassing past.[209]

> **The only thing necessary for the triumph of evil is for good men** [and women] **to do nothing.** Edmund Burke (1729–1797), attributed

It is time for people to decide whether they are for democracy or not. If we are for it, then we must surely be "for it" at the global level, and we have to improve it with whatever corruption-proofing or "transparency" measures and technologies are available to us. And if we are for democracy at the global level, we must face the disturbing fact that we don't have it yet, and recognize that we now know exactly what we have to do to get it. I hope for the sake of all that we are up to this historic challenge. I call upon

---

[208] Its past impotence is perhaps best described by General Roméo Dallaire (now a Canadian Senator) in his book *Shake Hands with the Devil* (now a feature film), in which he tells of his time in Rwanda, charged with stopping genocide but denied the mandate, equipment and boots on the ground to do his job by the cowardice and dithering of his UN masters.

[209] It may turn out to be a bit like quitting cigarettes; it is really hard at first, but it gradually gets easier until you finally reach a really nice new "normal" where you hardly remember that you ever smoked at all. People don't sit around today wistfully wishing that they could see a human sacrifice, or wishing they could buy a couple of slaves or behead a really annoying neighbour, do they? No, but our ancestors did, almost as a full-time job. We are *so over* all that.

every person, every government and every other institution in the world to support this effort in whatever ways they are able.

> **Hearken not to the voice which petulantly tells you that the form of government recommended ... is impossible to accomplish.** James Madison, No. 14 of *The Federalist Papers*, 1787-88 (all 85 essays were published under the pen name Publius)

If you haven't done this yet, please go now to www.voteworldgovernment.org and cast your vote in the global referendum on democratic world government, then contact your friends and family and ask them to do likewise.

Appendix #1

Public opinion on global governance

This survey was conducted for the International Secretariat of the World Social Forum by GlobeScan in December of 2004. The report was in the *Global Issues Monitor*, which was sent to the author by email. Here is that person's expression of the question that was asked in this poll. The *Global Issues Monitor* is a private and costly service, and although we were unable to confirm the precise wording of the question, we have found no reason to doubt the wording below.

Do you favor or oppose the creation of a new UN Parliament made up of representatives directly-elected by citizens and equivalent to the UN General Assembly?

COUNTRY	FAVOR %	OPPOSE %
Mexico	80	5
Brazil	73	10
Indonesia	73	13
Italy	70	20
China	68	20
Argentina	66	6
Germany	66	24
Canada	65	28
Philippines	65	29
Chile	64	8
Great Britain	64	28
South Korea	62	33
Poland	59	9
India	56	22
Australia	56	35
Turkey	55	18
USA	55	35
Russia	33	22
Average	**63**	**20**

Depends / Neither / Don't know / No answer 17%

Appendix #2

Draft United Nations Resolution
for a
Global Referendum
on
Democratic World Government

THE GENERAL ASSEMBLY,

EXPRESSING deep concern over the danger of nuclear war and the danger that WMD (weapons of mass destruction) may be used by non-national groups, either of which could imperil the existence of life on Earth,

MINDFUL of the profound problems (climate change, HIV/AIDS, etc.) that persist and worsen for lack of resources while more than one trillion (1,000 billion) dollars are spent on armaments every year,

BEARING IN MIND that all nations and all people need genuine security in the age of "overkill" weapons, and that real security is now possible only through the establishment of an effective and widely supported world authority,

AFFIRMING the interest of all individuals in expressing their preferences on a matter as fundamental as the survival of humankind, and indeed asserting a human right on the part of all adults to participate meaningfully in such a basic choice,

RESPECTING the principle of subsidiarity, whereby issues are handled by the lowest appropriate level of government, thus leaving national issues to national governments, local issues to municipal governments, and so on,

REALIZING that people of every background would be inclined to support the creation of a directly-elected world parliament that is empowered to adopt and enforce legislation on such supranational issues as security, justice, peace, and the protection of the shared natural environment,

RECALLING that Article 21 of the *Universal Declaration of Human Rights* provides that "The will of the people shall be the basis of the authority of government [and that] this will shall be expressed in periodic and genuine elections which ... shall be held by secret vote or by equivalent free voting procedures,"

KNOWING that because the will of the people is the basis of all political power and authority, a clear expression of that will in a mandate emerging from a successful global referendum must be given effect to by all national governments,

ACCEPTING that the above principles find strong support in the *Declaration on the Inadmissibility of Intervention in the Domestic Affairs of States and the Protection of their Independence and Sovereignty*, whose Preamble states that: "... all peoples have an inalienable right to ... the exercise of their sovereignty ... and that, by virtue of that right, they freely determine their political status,"

REALIZING that a substantial mandate from the people of all nations would provide a compelling base of legal and political   support for the establishment of a democratic world government to effectively address threats posed to humankind, such as weapons of mass destruction and environmental degradation,

DETERMINED to provide to all adult human beings the opportunity to formally express their views on this matter,

1. **RESOLVES** to seek the unanimous agreement of all Member States to a brief and simple expression of the goal of Democratic World Government;

2. **DECIDES** to use this wording: **"Do you support the creation of a directly-elected, representative and democratic world government?"** on the ballot in a Global Referendum;

3. **CALLS UPON** each Member Nation to voluntarily collect its "national component" of the Global Referendum before January 1, 2018;

4. **ENCOURAGES** each Member Nation to seek full and open debate of all sides of the issue prior to holding the vote among its national population;

5. **DETERMINES** that no one may cast a ballot before having attained the age of sixteen;

6. **RESOLVES** that the collection of each "national component" of the Global Referendum must be accompanied by minimum United Nations supervision to ensure the fairness of the voting procedures; and

7. **DECIDES** to form a committee to study the idea of a Global Referendum on Democratic World Government, and report back to the next Session of the General Assembly.

* * *

A curious historical note: While the GlobeScan Poll (Appendix #1) indicates that global public opinion is about 75% in favour of a UN parliament or a world government, and while most people expect American public opinion to run against the proposal discussed herein, more than half a century ago, there was a referendum in a U.S. state, piggybacked onto the 1948 elections, and it was a landslide *in favour* of world government! An article by Joseph Lyford, "Vote For World Government," from the *New Republic*, December 12, 1948 (in David Christensen's book *Healing the World*) describes it thus:

> On the day after the election, the commentators were too busy explaining that Harry Truman was still President to pay any attention to an interesting political development in the state of Connecticut. Along with the newspapers, they ignored what turned out to be the only real landslide victory in the nation. The victor in this one-sided election contest was, oddly enough, not a candidate for public office. It was a referendum proposal to change the United Nations into a limited World Government, and it won by a vote of 130,548 to 11,467—an almost 12-to-1 margin.

Christensen notes that Connecticut's remarkable news was overshadowed by President Harry Truman's surprise victory over New York Governor Thomas Dewey.

Appendix #3

PROPOSED REPRESENTATION OF PEOPLE
BY CONSTITUENCY AND BY COUNTRY
AT THE DEMOCRATIC WORLD GOVERNMENT

Below is a chart showing how "representation by population" would apply to the DWG. The first column has the names of all nations, in alphabetical order. The second column has the national population of the country, counted in millions. The third column shows the number of constituencies in that nation, assuming one constituency per 10 million people (or a part thereof). Any country with less than 10 million citizens would still have a member of the global parliament (MGP) with at least one vote. Even if a national population is less than one million, they still get one MGP and one vote.[210] So, an MGP gets a minimum of one vote to a maximum of ten votes in the DWG. If there is a nation with 11 million people, for example, it would elect 2 MGPs, and each would get 5.5 votes in the DWG. Since there is one MGP per constituency, the figure in column #3 is both the number of constituencies *and the number of MGPs* for that country. Column #4 shows the number of votes per MGP in that country, using a weighted voting system (one vote per million people in a constituency, or major part thereof).

We will assume that the DWG will have *about* 700 MGPs, since by 2018 (our target date for the opening of the DWG) the world population should be *about* 7 billion. We will have to ask all national governments (and their ambassadors at the UN) to help in the effort to define the boundaries of DWG constituencies fairly, and to at least consider finishing the global referendum themselves by adding the DWG referendum question to the ballot at the time of their next national elections.

---

[210] If everything worked out neatly and the world could be divided into equal constituencies all exactly of ten million people, we'd have 700 MGPs with 7000 votes in the DWG in 2018. However, with all these ways of dividing things up, we may have 738+ MGPs and 7,038+ votes (see Chapter 8). It should be said that with so many votes (7,038+) in play at the DWG, we don't have to worry about undue influence of the 38 tiny nations that have populations of less than one million. If any vote is razor thin and this issue becomes critical, their votes can be factored down according to their populations to make an average of one vote per *actual* million people.

Representation of people within countries in the democratic world government

1	2	3	4
Countries (in alphabetical order)	**Population** in millions <u>and</u> **# of DWG votes**	**Number of constituencies** and **MGPs**	**Number of votes per MGP**
1 Afghanistan	29	3	(29 ÷ 3 =) 9.7
2 Albania	4	1	4
3 Algeria	32	4	8
4 Andorra	0.07	1	1
5 Angola	11	2	5.5
6 Antigua and Barbuda	0.07	1	1
7 Argentina	39	4	9.75
8 Armenia	3	1	3
9 Australia	20	2	10
10 Austria	8	1	8
11 Azerbaijan	8	1	8
12 Bahamas	0.3	1	1
13 Bahrain	0.7	1	1
14 Bangladesh	142	15	9.5
15 Barbados	0.3	1	1
16 Belarus	10	1	10
17 Belgium	10	1	10
18 Belize	0.3	1	1
19 Benin	7	1	7
20 Bhutan	2	1	2
21 Bolivia	9	1	9
22 Bosnia and Herzegovina	4	1	4
23 Botswana	2	1	2
24 Brazil	184	19	9.7
25 Brunei	0.4	1	1
26 Bulgaria	8	1	8
27 Burkina Faso	14	2	7
28 Burundi	6	1	6
29 Cambodia	13	2	6.5
30 Cameroon	16	2	8
31 Canada	33	4	8.25
32 Cape Verde	0.4	1	1
33 Central African Republic	4	1	4

Countries (in alphabetical order)	Population in millions and # of DWG votes	Number of constituencies and MGPs	Number of votes per MGP
34 Chad	10	1	10
35 Chile	16	2	8
36 China	1,299	130	10
37 Colombia	42	5	8.5
38 Comoros	0.7	1	1
39 Democratic Republic of the Congo	58	6	9.5
40 Republic of the Congo	3	1	3
41 Costa Rica	4	1	4
42 Cote D'Ivoire	17	2	8.5
43 Croatia	4	1	4
44 Cuba	11	2	5.5
45 Cyprus	0.8	1	1
46 Czech Republic	10	1	10
47 Denmark	5	1	5
48 Djibouti	0.5	1	1
49 Dominica	0.07	1	1
50 Dominican Republic	9	1	9
51 East Timor	1	1	1
52 Ecuador	13	2	6.5
53 Egypt	76	8	9.5
54 El Salvador	7	1	7
55 Equatorial Guinea	0.5	1	1
56 Eritrea	4	1	4
57 Estonia	1	1	1
58 Ethiopia	68	7	9.7
59 Fiji	1	1	1
60 Finland	5	1	5
61 France	60	6	10
62 Gabon	1	1	1
63 Gambia	2	1	2
64 Georgia	5	1	5
65 Germany	82	9	9.1
66 Ghana	21	3	7
67 Greece	11	2	5.5

Countries (in alphabetical order)	Population in millions and # of DWG votes	Number of constituencies and MGPs	Number of votes per MGP
68 Grenada	0.1	1	1
69 Guatemala	14	2	7
70 Guinea	9	1	9
71 Guinea-Bissau	1	1	1
72 Guyana	0.7	1	1
73 Haiti	8	1	8
74 Holy See (Vatican City)	0.01	(Has observer status at UN)	
75 Honduras	7	1	7
76 Hungary	10	1	10
77 Iceland	0.3	1	1
78 India	1,065	107	10
79 Indonesia	239	24	10
80 Iran	69	7	10
81 Iraq	25	3	8.4
82 Ireland	4	1	4
83 Israel	6	1	6
84 Italy	58	6	9.6
85 Jamaica	3	1	3
86 Japan	127	13	9.8
87 Jordan	6	1	6
88 Kazakhstan	15	2	7.5
89 Kenya	32	4	8
90 Kiribati	0.1	1	1
91 Korea (N)	23	3	7.7
92 Korea (S)	49	5	10
93 Kuwait	2	1	2
94 Kyrgyzstan	5	1	5
95 Laos	6	1	6
96 Latvia	2	1	2
97 Lebanon	4	1	4
98 Lesotho	2	1	2
99 Liberia	3	1	3
100 Libya	6	1	6
101 Liechtenstein	0.03	1	1
102 Lithuania	4	1	4
103 Luxembourg	0.5	1	1
104 Macedonia	2	1	2
105 Madagascar	18	2	9
106 Malawi	12	2	6

Countries (in alphabetical order)	Population in millions and # of DWG votes	Number of constituencies and MGPs	Number of votes per MGP
107 Malaysia	24	3	8
108 Maldives	0.3	1	1
109 Mali	12	2	6
110 Malta	0.4	1	1
111 Marshall Islands	0.05	1	1
112 Mauritania	3	1	3
113 Mauritius	1	1	1
114 Mexico	105	11	9.5
115 Micronesia	0.1	1	1
116 Moldova	4	1	4
117 Monaco	0.03	1	1
118 Mongolia	3	1	3
119 Montenegro	0.7	1	1
120 Morocco	32	4	8
121 Mozambique	19	2	9.5
122 Myanmar	43	5	8.5
123 Namibia	2	1	2
124 Nauru	0.01	1	1
125 Nepal	27	3	9
126 Netherlands	16	2	8
127 New Zealand	4	1	4
128 Nicaragua	5	1	5
129 Niger	11	2	5.5
130 Nigeria	137	14	9.8
131 Norway	5	1	5
132 Oman	3	1	3
133 Pakistan	159	16	10
134 Palau	0.02	1	1
135 Panama	3	1	3
136 Papua New Guinea	5	1	5
137 Paraguay	6	1	6
138 Peru	28	3	9.3
139 Philippines	86	9	9.6
140 Poland	39	4	10
141 Portugal	11	2	5.5
142 Qatar	0.8	1	1
143 Romania	22	3	7.3
144 Russia	144	15	9.6
145 Rwanda	8	1	8

Countries (in alphabetical order)	Population in millions and # of DWG votes	Number of constituencies and MGPs	Number of votes per MGP
146 St Kitts and Nevis	0.04	1	1
147 St Lucia	0.2	1	1
148 St Vincent and the Grenadines	0.1	1	1
149 Samoa	0.2	1	1
150 San Marino	0.03	1	1
151 Sao Tome and Principe	0.2	1	1
152 Saudi Arabia	26	3	8.7
153 Senegal	11	2	5.5
154 Serbia	10	1	10
155 Seychelles	0.08	1	1
156 Sierra Leone	6	1	6
157 Singapore	4	1	4
158 Slovakia	5	1	5
159 Slovenia	2	1	2
160 Solomon Islands	0.5	1	1
161 Somalia	8	1	8
162 South Africa	43	5	8.6
163 Spain	40	4	10
164 Sri Lanka	20	2	10
165 Sudan	39	4	9.8
166 Suriname	0.5	1	1
167 Swaziland	1	1	1
168 Sweden	9	1	9
169 Switzerland	7	1	7
170 Syria	18	2	9
171 Taiwan	23	3	7.7
172 Tajikistan	7	1	7
173 Tanzania	37	4	9.3
174 Thailand	65	7	9.3
175 Togo	6	1	6
176 Tonga	0.1	1	1
177 Trinidad and Tobago	1	1	1
178 Tunisia	10	1	10
179 Turkey	69	7	9.9
180 Turkmenistan	5	1	5
181 Tuvalu	0.01	1	1
182 Uganda	26	3	8.7

Countries (in alphabetical order)	Population in millions and # of DWG votes	Number of constituencies and MGPs	Number of votes per MGP
183 Ukraine	48	5	9.6
184 United Arab Emirates	3	1	3
185 United Kingdom	60	6	10
186 United States	300	30	10
187 Uruguay	3	1	3
188 Uzbekistan	26	3	8.7
189 Vanuatu	0.2	1	1
190 Venezuela	24	3	8
191 Vietnam	83	9	9.2
192 Yemen	20	2	10
193 Zambia	10	1	10
194 Zimbabwe	13	2	6.5

[NOTE: Several people asked me why I went to the trouble of working all of this out, even while admitting it was the most sensible way of arranging things. In truth, it wasn't much trouble, and it is, after all, the most sensible way of arranging things.]

Appendix #4

Below is an excerpt from the musical film *Camelot*, wherein King Arthur tries and fails to convince a crusty old knight (Pellinore) that laws and courts are better than bloodshed as the way to resolve conflicts and disputes. Today, people have learned this lesson at the municipal, provincial and national level; now we must learn it on the global level.

Transcript of a scene from the musical film "Camelot"

ARTHUR: It is simple, Pellinore, once you get it into that armoured head of yours, that all disputes would be settled by law, and not by bloodshed.

PELLINORE: I understand that perfectly. I do *not* understand how it works.

ARTHUR: Oh Pelli. Suppose you are accused of burning down a stable.

PELLINORE: Whose?

ARTHUR: Let us say a farmer named William.

PELLINORE: William? Well, I wouldn't, of course, but … carry on.

ARTHUR: Now, Pelli, you claim you haven't [burned it down].

PELLINORE: Yes.

ARTHUR: What does he do?

PELLINORE: Well, he holds his tongue if he knows what's good for him, or he'll get a sword through the chest.

ARTHUR: Oh, Pelli. Pelli, he … takes you to court!

PELLINORE: Ah! And we fight there.

ARTHUR: No, Pellinore. In court, there is a prosecutor for farmer William, and a defender for you.

PELLINORE: Oh! I see! I see! And *they* fight!

ARTHUR: No, Pellinore. A *jury* decides. That is why it is called "trial by jury."

PELLINORE: A jury? Who in thunderation are they? It's none of their damn business in the first place.

ARTHUR: But you don't know them, Pelli, and they don't know you.

PELLINORE: But if they don't know me and they don't know farmer William, how can you expect them to care a fig who wins? How can you get a fair decision from people [who are] so impartial?

ARTHUR: That ... is precisely the point, Pelli. They are impartial ... and there will be no bloodshed.

PELLINORE: Oh. Well I'll tell you something. If that jury finds me guilty, there'll be plenty of bloodshed. I'll have a whack at every last one of them.

ARTHUR: Then you will be charged with murder, Pelli.

PELLINORE: Why the ruddy thing's endless! Another jury finds me guilty, and I'll have to have a whack at them! And so on and so on and ... oh!

ARTHUR: Pellinore, forget it! You will never burn down a stable, and you will never know a farmer named William, and you will never ever *ever* be found in a court!

PELLINORE: Not without my ruddy sword, I won't. Sheesh!

Appendix #5

Hoped-for sequence of events

Below is a chart showing the main issues from start to finish on an anticipated and hoped-for timeline. Note the overlap of events.

TIME → EVENT ↓	2007	'08	'09	'10	'11	'12	'13	'14	'15	'16	'17	'18	'19+
Online voting continues	'05 → → → → → → → → → → → → → →))))))))))))))))))))))))))))))))))) [until no longer needed]												
Preliminary constitution draft work			→ → → → →)))))))))))))))))) [start point depends on finances and other resources]										
Electoral commission set up						→ → → → → → →))))))))))))))))))))))))))) [constitution work; constituency boundary disputes settled]							
National referenda begin						→ → → → → → →)))))))))))))))))))))) [start point depends largely on success of UN resolution]							
Draft constitution finalized								→ → → →)))))))))))))) [or later, if draft constitution not ready]					
Global general election											→ →)))))) [Members of the Global Parliament elected, and go to work]		
World constitution referendum											→ →)))))) [with the global election; later, if a draft constitution not ready]		
Inaugural session of full DWG												→ →)))))) [assuming global general election is largely completed]	

What we think the vote count could and should be in this decade (2008 to 2018). These are guesses; they could be high *or low*.

2008	2009	2010	2011	2012
500,000	1 million	5 million	20 million	50 million

2013	2014	2015	2016	2017
100 million	400 million	1 billion	2 billion+	**WE WIN**

Appendix #6

One proposed world constitution (summary)

Reproduced with permission from David Christensen's book *Healing the World: A Primer About the World and How We Must Fix It For Our Children* (this is his APPENDIX F). He points out that all of the proposed world constitutions that have already been developed may prove useful as first drafts when a true world constitutional framing conference is finally called.

* * *

Following are summary concepts from such a draft developed by a group of scholars led by Robert Hutchins, Chancellor of the University of Chicago, in 1948.

Summary concepts of the Hutchins draft of a World Constitution:

a. War must and can be outlawed and peace can and must be universally enacted and enforced;

b. World Government is the only alternative to world destruction;

c. "World Government is necessary, therefore it is possible";

d. The price of World Government and peace is justice.

The Hutchins group proposed a "Federal Republic of the World." Beginning with its dedication to Mahatma Ghandi and a "Declaration of Duties and Rights" of world citizens, it acknowledged that "the four elements of life—earth, water, air, energy—are the common property of the human race."

The Hutchins group proposed a Federal Convention made up of delegates directly by the people of all nations, the numbers based on population. The Federal Convention [is] to be divided into 9 regional "Electoral Colleges" of "kindred nations and cultures." Delegates would vote as individuals, not as representatives of their respective nations or Electoral Colleges, and they should select representatives for the World Council. The World Council would be the legislative body.

Other elements of the Hutchins group proposal were: a President, an executive Chancellor with a Cabinet, a Supreme Court, a Tribune (who would function as spokesperson for minorities), and a Chamber of Guardians (whose duties would be to maintain the peace and direct a military unit).

Bibliography

The Weather Makers by Tim Flannery

The Anatomy of Peace by Emery Reves

World Peace Through World Law by Grenville Clark and Louis B. Sohn

The Age of Consent, A Manifesto for a New World Order by George Monbiot

One World Democracy by Jerry Tetalman and Byron Belitsos

A Global Parliament: Principles of World Federation by Dr. Chris Hamer

Humanity or Sovereignty, by Lyndon Storey

The Second Superpower, Extreme Democracy by James F. Moore

The Great Turning: From Empire to Earth Community by David Korten

Globalizar la Democracia: por un Parlamento Mundial by Fernando A. Inglesias (available only in Spanish for now)

"Towards a Global Parliament," an article by Richard Falk and Andrew Strauss, *The Nation* magazine, September 23, 2003

"The Mirage of UN Reform," an article by Harold S. Bidmead

The World Must be Governed, Vernon Nash

Healing the World: A Primer About the World and How We Must Fix It For Our Children, David E. Christensen

Tilting at Windbags: The Autobiography of a World Federalist, Harold S. Bidmead

Parliament of Man, Harold S. Bidmead

Looking for Square Two – To a Better and Safer World, Douglas Mattern

Earth Charter, http://en.wikipedia.org/wiki/Earth_Charter

Forms and materials

What follows are some materials **to help you get started on your own DWG campaign.** *Photocopy materials from book, then use.*

Page 184   Printed ballot, for those with no Internet access

Page 185   Small poster (6" by 9") about democratic world government and the idea of a global referendum

Page 186   Card-sized notices – photocopy the page, use scissors or paper cutter to cut off the black box lines then hand them out at will

Page 187   Tabbed poster – photocopy the page, use scissors to cut up from the bottom between the tabs so they are easily torn off, then tack or tape the page onto public bulletin boards

Printed ballot

Do you support the creation of a directly-elected, representative and democratic world government?

YES ☐   Check one box only   **NO** ☐

Only your **first** name, your country and how you voted will be posted on the Internet, but we need the additional information to try to protect the integrity of the voting process. Please fill in all of the boxes below.

Given name (no nicknames please)	required
Family name (surname)	required
Street address	required
City or town	required
State or Province	<u>not</u> required
Postal or Zip Code	required
Country	required
Date of Birth (month, day and year) (must be 16+ to vote)	required
Email address (yours or a contact)	<u>not</u> required

<u>PLEASE NOTE</u>: This paper ballot will be submitted to VWG.org by way of the Internet by one of our volunteers. Your vote will be assigned a number as its ID, and this ID will be posted on the Internet with your vote as soon as we have your vote. If you want to know this ID number to show to a family member later, for instance, or just for your records, ask our volunteer for it, and he or she will look it up and give it to you. (Since these ID numbers are assigned to ballots in the order that they are received, the ID number of your vote is also *approximately* the number of people who voted before you.)

If you want to send your filled-in ballot by mail, our address is Vote World Government, Box 1102, Shawville, QC, Canada, J0X 2Y0

For more, our site is www.voteworldgovernment.org. You can vote online if you prefer.

<u>Earth Needs a Democratic World Government</u>

www.voteworldgovernment.org

1. Within any nation, the choice is between government (the rule of law) and anarchy (the law of the jungle).

2. While no government is perfect, serious people reject anarchy.

3. Governments are either democratic or dictatorial. Given a voice in the matter, the people of every nation will choose democracy, overwhelmingly.

These three statements are also true *for the world as a whole*. Without a world government to make world laws, nations will continue to make war, and terrorists will continue to kill innocent civilians for political gain. With nuclear, chemical and biological weapons in the mix, a World War III may well destroy all life on Earth. At some level, most people already know these things, but they incorrectly think they are helpless to change anything.

The United Nations is mostly a **gathering place of national governments**. It is not, and will never become, the democratic world government that we need. We believe that by **using the Internet** and working with all levels of government and the UN, we can conduct a **global referendum** (or at least kick-start the process), and obtain a **strong mandate** from the **entire human race** for the creation of a directly-elected **world parliament** that will be empowered to resolve international conflicts lawfully. The test is whether the **mandate** will prove to be **"legally binding"** on national governments. We think it will, and we think that this is what it will take if future generations are to live out their lives **without experiencing war or environmental collapse**, and if we are to create the political conditions under which humans can survive *and thrive* for **millions of years into the future**.

Visit www.voteworldgovernment.org to cast your vote or learn more.

[PHOTOCOPY PAGE, CUT OUT THE CARDS BY CUTTING OFF THE BLACK LINES WITH
SCISSORS, CARRY SOME IN YOUR WALLET AND HAND THEM OUT]

Democratic World Government

through a global referendum

Is it time to create a directly-
elected, democratic government
for the world?

Many people think it is.

Visit
www.voteworldgovernment.org
to learn more or to cast your vote.

Democratic World Government

through a global referendum

Is it time to create a directly-
elected, democratic government
for the world?

Many people think it is.

Visit
www.voteworldgovernment.org
to learn more or to cast your vote.

Democratic World Government

through a global referendum

Is it time to create a directly-
elected, democratic government
for the world?

Many people think it is.

Visit
www.voteworldgovernment.org
to learn more or to cast your vote.

Democratic World Government

through a global referendum

Is it time to create a directly-
elected, democratic government
for the world?

Many people think it is.

Visit
www.voteworldgovernment.org
to learn more or to cast your vote.

Earth is in grave danger, and it's our fault!

If you think the time is right to set up a democratic world government, go to www.voteworldgovernment.org

AND VOTE TODAY

**You CAN make a difference.
Get your friends and family to vote too.**

Poster created by Vote World Government, a non-profit organization registered in Québec, Canada as VWG.org. Volunteers are asked to photocopy this page, trim it, cut upwards in between the tabs below and post (**just where posting is allowed**).

www.voteworldgovernment.org
www.voteworldgovernment.org
www.voteworldgovernment.org
www.voteworldgovernment.org
www.voteworldgovernment.org
www.voteworldgovernment.org
www.voteworldgovernment.org
www.voteworldgovernment.org

INDEX